CHILD DEVELOPMENT

VOLUME ONE

A Systematic and Empirical Theory

CHILD DEVELOPMENT

VOLUME ONE

A Systematic and Empirical Theory

BY

Sidney W. Bijou
UNIVERSITY OF ILLINOIS
AND
Donald M. Baer
KANSAS UNIVERSITY

New York

APPLETON-CENTURY-CROFTS

Educational Division

MEREDITH CORPORATION

Copyright © 1961 by
APPLETON-CENTURY-CROFTS, INC.

741-14

Library of Congress Card Number: 61-14365

PRINTED IN THE UNITED STATES OF AMERICA
390-09263-0

PREFACE

It might be said that this volume represents an "extended learning theory" or an "empirical behavior theory" of human psychological development. To a degree, these terms are accurate. However, they have had such varied use in psychological writing that their meanings have become obscured by controversy. In fact, use of these terms no longer insures an accurate statement of the approach, coverage, or subject matter of any theory. Consequently, rather than add to the clutter of meaning attached to these words, we find it better to describe this volume as a systematic and empirical theory of human psychological development from the point of view of natural science. These terms are defined in the Introduction of the text. To the reader who looks upon the approach of natural science as the basic method of knowledge, this treatment will simply be an extension of that approach to the analysis of what is popularly called "child psychology." To the reader who holds a different view of the nature of theory, perhaps this work may offer an example of an alternative approach. And for the reader with no particular outlook on the methodological problem of what constitutes a scientific statement, this volume will at least provide a set of concepts and principles useful in the description and organization of child behavior and development. We would add that this system of concepts also offers a significant degree of *explanation*.

This volume is written for the college student who is interested in child behavior and development and has little or no background in psychology. Consequently, we have included only the most basic terms and principles. Those details of learning mechanisms which generate so much heat among learning theorists have been largely omitted. Those descriptions of the phenomena of learning and behavior change which are common to all of their arguments have been retained, stated in terms designed to be simple, clear, and complete. In particular, these terms are as nontechnical as possible, and the examples supporting each concept are intended to clarify and generalize its meaning, not to document its validity.

In fact, no attempt is made to document these principles. Occasional references to research findings are for illustrative purposes. This decision is based on three considerations. First, an attempt to validate these concepts would be contrary to the objective of presenting an easily readable account of the theory itself. The presentation would have to be longer, more complex, and certainly much more technical. Second, the data upon which a theory like this is built are well summarized in several texts designed for that purpose. Some of these are noted in our reference list. Third, pertinent references to the literature of psychological development are included in the succeeding volumes.

This volume is the first in a series. The others analyze child behavior and development in terms of the theory presented here. They are organized into the most clearly discernible stages of psychological development, infancy, childhood, and adolescence.

Essentially, this theory merely brings together in a specific application the conceptual contributions of many psychologists. Our most basic debts are to B. F. Skinner, J. R. Kantor, F. S. Keller, and W. N. Schoenfeld. We hope that this application of their work will give additional impetus to the objective analysis of human behavior.

Also, we wish to thank our students and colleagues for their helpful comments and criticism. With respect to the latter, we are particularly indebted to Jay Birnbrauer, Howard C. Gilhousen, Wendell E. Jeffrey, Lewis P. Lipsitt, and O. Ivar Lovaas. Our special appreciation is due Kenneth MacCorquodale, Assistant Editor of the Century Psychology Series, for his assistance.

Finally, we wish to express our gratitude to the Department of Health, Education, and Welfare for Public Health Service grants M-2208 and M-2232. Much of this volume is our response to the problems we have investigated with the support of their grants.

S.W.B
D.M.B

CONTENTS

CHILD DEVELOPMENT

VOLUME ONE

*A Systematic and
Empirical Theory*

Introduction

We present here an approach to the understanding of human psychological development from the natural science point of view. Our presentation is in the form of a theory. We shall pave the way for an explanation of the theory by examining and clarifying what is meant by the key terms of our objective: "psychological development," "natural science," and "theory."

By "psychological development" we mean progressive changes in the way an organism's behavior interacts with the environment. An *interaction* between behavior and environment means simply that a given response may be expected to occur or not, depending on the stimulation the environment provides. We may also expect that if the response does occur, it will somehow change the environment and its stimulus properties. This change in environmental stimulation may cause another response to occur; this response too may be expected to effect some changes in the environment; and so on. For example, a man may be driving his car on a cloudy day. Suddenly, the sun breaks through the clouds—a change in environmental stimulation. The bright light causes the man to squint, a response which reduces the glare. Squinting requires too much effort for comfort, and reduces the driver's field of vision. These two response-produced changes in stimulation, the strain of partly closing the eyes and the restriction of visibility, lead him to respond further by reaching for his sunglasses in the glove compartment.

This example shows that behavior is in constant interaction with the stimulus environment. The subject matter of this discussion, however, is psychological *development,* that is, progressive *changes* in such interactions which occur with the passage of time between conception and death. Typically, our interest will be in changes over periods of months and years. Take the behavior of eating as an example. Eating is a fairly well-defined series of responses and stimuli in interaction. For the infant, this interaction involves stimulation by the sight and feel of the breast, and by the length of time elapsed since the last feeding. Let us assume that four hours have elapsed since the infant's last meal. Under these circumstances the sight of mother's breast or the feel of her nipple against his cheek gives rise to a sucking response. The effect of sucking behavior is to supply food, and the effect of this new state of affairs is to decrease sucking, which gives rise to other responses (looking about, smiling, gurgling, going to sleep, etc.). But for the toddler, eating is in many ways a different interaction. Again, the length of time since the last meal is an important stimulus condition, but now the sight and feel of mother's breast as a stimulus for eating have been replaced by the sight, feel, and smell of things like cereal, milk, juice, dishes, spoons, and cups. The response is no longer sucking, but is instead a series of reaching, grasping, and bringing-to-the-mouth responses, all of which provide a stimulation to gums and tongue which gives rise to chewing and swallowing rather than sucking. The end result is still the same: a change from a situation without food to one with an ample amount; but this change is likely to be followed by responses rather different from those seen in the infant—much more complex behaviors of looking about and vocalizing, perhaps crying to be let out of the baby table or high chair, and a much smaller probability of dropping off to sleep.

Thus, eating in infants is one interaction, and eating in toddlers is another, with many elements changed. It is exactly the changes in these elements which are our primary concern here. How and why do they come about? Our answers to this question, and to all other questions about changing interactions between behavior and environment with increasing age and experience, will make up the body of *this* volume. In general, the answers will involve changes in the child's environment, changes in his ability to respond, and the interactions between them. For example, when a child has sufficient response capability (is well able to walk and run, is reliably toilet trained, has a fair vocabulary, is reasonably manageable by strangers) we change his environment drastically by sending him to school. There, many of his old interactions change, and many entirely new interactions are developed. Thus, changes in the way in which human behavior interacts with the stimulus environment is the basic concern in all that is to follow.

A second key term in our statement of purpose is *theory*. By *theory* we mean one of the several definitions given in the 1958 edition of *Webster's Collegiate Dictionary:* ". . . the general or abstract principles of any body of facts." Thus a theory of psychological development consists of a set of statements which show the general environment-behavior relationships which summarize the particular interactions we observe in the child. So a theoretical statement would not be simply a statement of some particular interaction, such as the way a toddler named Johnny eats. Instead, it would be a statement about many such particular interactions, tying them all together in some way so that they exemplify a general principle of development. For example, we might explain why, in general, toddlers learn to eat with a spoon. This is because mothers consistently feed toddlers with a spoon, and so one is always present at mealtimes and often is available for picking up. Toddlers in general do pick things up and put them in their mouths. When those things have food on them, the same response is more likely to occur again. Here we are making a statement of principles, which shows the essential similarity of the eating situation of a great number of particular toddlers, introduces a principle of learning based on food, and thus explains why toddlers generally learn to eat with spoons.

The third key term in our statement of purpose, *natural science*, is closely related to the meaning of theory used here. Natural science is the study of any natural phenomenon (i.e., of any lawful, orderly phenomenon) by certain methods. These are the methods which characterize the scientist and distinguish him from other people who also seek knowledge about the same phenomena by different methods. The philosopher, for example, may gain knowledge by reflecting upon statements which seem fundamental and unquestionable to him, and then by deducing from these premises conclusions about particular problems. The artist may simply reflect his inner feelings in words, verse, painting, sculpture, or music as the artistic truth (at least for him) about any problem. But the scientist (as we define him) restricts himself to a study of what he can observe. His general procedure is to manipulate in an observable way whatever conditions he suspects are important to his problem, and then to observe what changes take place in the phenomenon as a result. These changes in the phenomenon he relates to his manipulation of conditions as orderly interactions: the speed of a falling body depends upon the length of time since it was released; the volume of a gas depends upon its temperature and the pressure exerted by its container; pulse rate depends upon breathing rate; the skill with which a toddler can eat with a spoon depends upon the number of times he has managed to get food in his mouth with it in past attempts.

The point to emphasize in this discussion is that the scientist deals with observable events. It is, therefore, in the tradition of natural science to say that the toddler develops skillful techniques of eating with a spoon largely because of his past success in getting food in his mouth that way. In general, responses that produce food grow stronger. All of this is observable. However, to say that the child learns this response because of an inner urge to grow up, or because he wants to be like adults, is to refer to something unobservable (an "urge," or a "want"); so, for us, this kind of statement is not consistent with scientific method.

This approach to science is one of several current in contemporary psychology. Clearly, we have made an arbitrary choice in choosing this definition rather than others which would permit statements about unobservable phenomena. We can point out as advantages the simplicity of this approach, its frequent fruitfulness, and its freedom from logical tangles which ultimately turn out to be illusory rather than real. Obviously, our usage of theory dovetails with this conception of science, since our theoretical statements are generalized summaries and explanations of observable interactions between behavior and the environment. Ultimately, evaluation of this usage of theory and science will depend upon the adequacy of its results in explaining our present problem, the psychological development of the organism.

2

The Context of Developmental Theory

A theory of human psychological development will involve a generalized description of the data of development and a statement of the relationships among these descriptive terms. In accordance with our objective of maintaining a natural science approach, our terms will be limited to the observable, recordable instances of the responses of the developing child, and to the specific events which operate on him and thus make up his environment. To help integrate this with material in other areas in psychology and closely related fields, we begin with a brief description of contemporary psychology, and indicate the relationship between psychology and animal biology on the one hand, and psychology and cultural anthropology on the other.

THE NATURE OF CONTEMPORARY PSYCHOLOGY

Psychology is one of the specializations of the general scientific activity of our culture. It is that subdivision of scientific work which specializes in analyzing interactions of responses of organisms and environmental events. We know, however, that other branches of science are also interested in responses and stimuli. What differentiates the psychologist's interest from others'?

With regard to *responses,* one difference is this: psychology is concerned with "the observable activity of the organism, as it moves about, stands still, seizes objects, pushes and pulls, makes sounds, gestures, and so on."[1] (In some instances, such observa-

[1] B. F. Skinner. *Cumulative record.* New York: Appleton-Century-Crofts, Inc., 1959, p. 205.

tions are impossible without special instruments. High-speed motion picture machines, tape recorders, timers, counters, and "lie detectors" are a few of the more familiar devices.) In other words, psychology concentrates on the organism as a unit of integrated responses. To say that psychology is concerned with the responses of a total functioning organism does not mean that a psychological study must attempt to observe and measure all responses taking place at one time. On the contrary, studies that have made the most basic contributions to behavioral science have focused on one or two measures as indices of total change. In practice, the number and kind of responses observed and the size of the stimulus-response interaction are dependent to a large extent on the objective of a particular study. In the sections to follow we shall say much more about the nature of and the interrelationships among psychological responses and their corresponding stimuli.

Stimulus events of especial interest to psychology are the physical, chemical, biological, and social events which *act on the individual.* "Some of these are to be found in the hereditary history of the individual, including his membership in a given species as well as his personal endowment. Others arise from his physical environment, past or present."[2] Such events may be observed and measured in two ways: by physical measuring devices (e.g., scales, rulers, and temperature gauges), and by measurement of changes in behavior produced by the stimulus (e.g., changes in the frequency, amplitude, or latency of some response). The latter method is of basic interest to psychology. The description and measurement of stimuli will be discussed in detail later.

It is obvious that the organism is continuously reacting to and is continuously being changed by stimuli. We have usually referred to these processes by terms such as learning, adjustment, maturation, growth, and adaptation. Furthermore, stimuli are always being acted upon and being changed by the behavior of the organism. Man is relentlessly concerned with changing the environment to enhance growth, development, and survival for himself and his posterity. Thus, stimulating conditions produce

[2] *Ibid.*, p. 206.

changes in behavior; these changes alter the environment; the altered environment (together with other influences such as the seasons of the year) produce further behaviors which again modify the environment, etc., etc., resulting in unique cultures (modified environments) on one hand, and individual psychological growth on the other.

At present, most psychologists concentrate on the phase of the stimuli-response interaction that is concerned with the modification of behavior as a consequence of stimulus events. This relationship is usually expressed thus: Behavior (B) is a function (f) of, or is a consequence of, stimulus events (S). It may be abbreviated this way:

$$B = f(S)$$

Stimuli, S, may conveniently be broken down into (1) stimuli acting currently, at the moment of observation, and (2) stimuli that have acted in the past (history). Then the elaborated form of the functional relationship takes the form:

$$B = f \begin{cases} (S_1) & \text{The current stimulus situation (physical, chemical, organismic, and social)} \\ (S_2) & \text{The history of stimulus situations (genetic inheritance and past events related to those in the current situation)} \end{cases}$$

This scheme of psychological analysis—behavior as a function of the current situation and history—should have a familiar ring. It is the one we frequently use in analyzing the behavior of others. The only new features here are the technical terminology and the systematic frame of reference.

Suppose that there are identical twin boys, four years of age, deeply engrossed in playing with cars and trucks. Suddenly, a pleasant, neat-appearing young lady opens the door, walks in, and closes the door. Both boys stop playing and look at her. Neither one has ever seen her before. One child gets up, scurries to the farthest corner and slinks behind a painting easel; the other, after a moment or two of further scrutiny, gets up and approaches the intruder with a smile. If you were asked to explain this difference in behavior, you would probably take into account the facts that both children have the same genes and that both were responding to roughly the same current stimulus situation when the young lady appeared. Probably we would conclude that the difference in their behavior is due to the differences in the past experiences (histories) of each child with young ladies resembling this one.

THE RELATIONSHIPS OF PSYCHOLOGY TO ANIMAL BIOLOGY AND CULTURAL ANTHROPOLOGY

It will clarify the domain of psychology to review its relationships to its two neighboring branches of science, animal (organismic) biology and cultural anthropology, in terms of our functional equation, $B = f(S)$. Animal biology is pertinent to both B and S variables, in general. Cultural anthropology is pertinent to S variables produced by the behavior of the members of the culture. Of course, the lines separating the fields are fuzzy. However, each field has certain discernible features, and each field is dependent on the other two for certain kinds of information. The features differentiating them are the ones we shall stress.

Animal biology may be defined as the study of the origin, reproduction, structure, and function of animal life. To a large extent this discipline is concerned with the interaction between organisms and organic and non-organic materials and with the consequent changes in the structure and functioning of their *parts*.[3] As we have said, psychology is primarily concerned with

[3] A noteworthy exception is that branch of biology known as *ecology*. Ecology deals with the relationships between the organism as a whole and its entire environment, which includes the existence and behavior of other organisms in that environment. As some ecologists have pointed out, this definition makes all of psychology, anthropology, sociology, history, economics, and political science mere subdivisions of ecology. (In practice, however, the ecologist often concentrates on such variables as the population of each species living in an environment, its food supply, and the effect of its changing numbers upon other species in the same environment.) This example re-emphasizes the overlapping nature of psychology, biology, and other sciences dealing with living organisms.

the interaction of an organism, as a *unified response system*, in relation to environmental events. It is apparent, therefore, that every psychological occurrence is itself a biological occurrence, that is, it is correlated with organismic events (interactions between parts of an organism and stimuli). Both sets of events take place simultaneously. Which set attracts the attention of an investigator depends primarily on whether his view of causation typically relates the entire organism to its controlling environment, or sees the entire organism as a complex sum of its separate parts. Either attitude is legitimate, but incomplete without the other. Some scientists have attempted to follow both viewpoints simultaneously, in both biology and psychology.

The behavior of an infant in feeding can serve as a case in point. From the psychological point of view, the important responses consist of grasping the nursing bottle, getting the nipple into the mouth, and sucking. It is necessary as well to take account of current environmental conditions (appearance, weight, and content of the bottle, convenience of the bottle for tiny hands, number of hours since last feeding, etc.) and of historical events (number of times in the past the sight of the bottle was followed by reaching, grasping, and thrusting the smaller end of the bottle into the mouth, producing milk; the typical number of hours between feedings, etc.). The same act might be studied from the organismic point of view in terms of the activity of the digestive system from the moment the milk contacts the infant's mouth to the time the waste products are eliminated.

The fact that psychological and organismic events take place at the same time does not mean that one class of events exclusively causes the other, that is, that organismic variables always cause psychological reactions, or vice versa. The causes (the related stimuli) of a specific phenomenon in either class, psychological or organismic, must be separately determined by an analysis of the specific environmental conditions which apply. Of course, organismic variables often do participate in determining psychological reactions just as psychological events often participate in producing organismic responses. (Indeed, the latter possibility is the main concern of psychosomatic medicine.) It will be recalled that on page 10 the environmental events of psychological behavior were said to include the organismic variables of central interest to the biologist. These stimuli, like the other important stimuli (physical, chemical, and social), *contribute* to causation. None of the four classes is necessarily singled out as the sole determinant for any psychological reaction. It is true, certainly, that for many psychological responses the main causal condition is organismic. For example, a sharp pain in the stomach from food poisoning may play the major role in producing the behaviors of clutching at the stomach and frantically telephoning the doctor. But in telephoning the doctor, it is obvious that a certain history of interaction with social stimuli is involved; otherwise the person would be unable to dial a telephone and would know nothing of doctors and their function in dealing with pain. Similarly, other psychological reactions are primarily caused by social stimuli ("You're welcome"), or by physical stimuli ("Ouch!"), or by chemical stimuli ("Phoo!"), but not by these alone.

However, in each instance of behavior, a properly complete account of the cause and effect relationships involved undoubtedly will include *all* classes of stimuli and their relevant interactional histories. Attending only to the dominant environmental event is bound to result in incomplete and oversimplified accounts of significant functional relationships. The occasionally encountered dictum that only motivation is causation in psychology is an example of a too restricted approach.

At the same time, to contend that biological events are not the sole or invariable causes of psychological events clearly does not diminish the interdependence of the two fields. Psychologists are interested in the findings of physiologists about the activities of the organs and systems of the human body that participate with other variables in determining psychological behavior. (For example, how does the hypothalamus mediate rage and anger?) Developmental psychologists seek from biologists information on the motor and sensory equipment of the child at various stages of development. (For example, are the taste buds of a preschool child anatomically comparable to those of an adult?) It should be apparent that prominent among the factors determining the occurrence of a response is the availability of the organismic equipment necessary to perform the act. (Learning to walk is partially dependent upon the strength of the leg bones and the relative weights of the head and torso.)

We turn now to a consideration of the relationships between psychology and the sciences concerned with social phenomenon, particularly cultural anthropology. Certainly the lion's share of the conditions determining psychological behavior is social in nature. These influences, which begin at birth and vary widely throughout the life span, include all the conditions involving people in some way. People make all sorts of demands ("Brush your teeth in the morning and again at night") and set all sorts of occasions for behavior ("It's time for lunch"); people approve behavior ("Atta boy!") and are present when social and physical hurts and restraints are removed ("You took that like a man"); people disapprove and punish behavior directly ("Go to the principal's office") and bring about non-social painful consequences ("You must open your mouth so the dentist can drill that tooth"); people prescribe the forms of behavior appropriate in significant social situations ("Put your napkin in your lap"), and set the level of skill required for tasks ("If your composition has more than one spelling error, you will flunk"); and people create many or most of the physical objects of the culture which play a part in shaping behavior.

Cultural anthropology, the study of man and the products of man, is devoted to analyzing social organizations, industrial techniques, art, religions, languages, laws, customs, and manners. Information about the origins, changes, and range of cultural events is indispensable to developmental psychology in relating social variables and behavior. For example, cultural anthropology analyzes adult—child and peer—child relationships, role specializations (mothering functions, provider of economic goods, head of local community, etc.), and social subgroupings (socio-economic class, urban-rural, and such) of a society. Another example, and an area of considerable current interest because of its promise to

shed more light on the formation of the patterns of social behavior ("personality"), concerns data on child-rearing practices
gathered in primitive as well as in complex societies. Specifically
these include mother and family activities in initiating an infant
into its society through the prescribed procedures involved in
feeding, toilet training, cleaning, dressing, sex training, and
aggression training.

3

The Nature of Developmental Theory

Developmental psychology is one of the major subdivisions of psychology, along with abnormal, social, comparative, and physiological psychology. Sometimes it is called genetic psychology since it is concerned with the origins and natural growth of behavior (this alternate designation should not be confused with genetics, that part of biological science dealing with the principles of heredity and variation in animals and plants). Developmental psychology specializes in studying the progressions in interactions between behavior and environmental events. In other words, it is concerned with the historical variables influencing behavior, that is, with the effect of past interactions on present interactions. In terms of the scheme for a functional analysis given on page 8 (behavior is a function of the events in the current situation and in the history of previous interactions), developmental psychology concentrates on *the history of an organism's previous interactions.*

To elaborate on the nature of developmental psychology, we shall extend our discussion of (1) the developing child, (2) the events in the environments of development, and (3) the interaction between the child and the environment. In other words, we shall go into greater detail on how the interaction between the child and environment may be analyzed from a natural science point of view.

THE DEVELOPING CHILD

The developing child may be adequately regarded, in conceptual terms, as a cluster of interrelated responses interacting with stimuli. Some of the stimuli emanate from the external environment, some from the child's own behavior, and some from his biological structure and functioning. The child is therefore not only a source of responses; he is also a source of some stimuli. From this point of view, part of the child's environment is within his own body.

The number and kinds of responses a child is capable of displaying at any point of his life are determined by his status in the animal kingdom (species characteristics), his biological maturational stage, and his history of interaction with his particular environment from fertilization on. On the face of it, the child makes a tremendous number and variety of separate reactions, and developmental psychologists have attempted to group them according to one or another conception of man's personality. Some have claimed that the child's external behaviors reveal one or another mental process, such as willing, feeling, or thinking; or reveal the growth and interactions of the id, ego, and superego parts of the personality. Others have viewed the child's observable behavior as consisting of motor, social, linguistic, emotional, and intellectual parts. It might be noted in passing that the last scheme attempts to analyze psychological behavior in terms of the functioning of several organic systems, just as biologists do in their studies of development (embryology). In the present treatment we propose to think of the developing child's behavior as being made up of two basic kinds of responses—*respondents* and *operants*.[1] Respondents are those responses which are controlled (strengthened or weakened) basically by stimuli that precede them, and operants are those responses which are controlled basically by the stimuli that follow them. This scheme will allow us to classify any response from the great diversity of a child's behavior into either of these two categories solely on the basis of objective, observable criteria. Such a distinction is functional or causal, in the sense that it is based on the variables, or stimuli, which control the response in question. This two-fold functional view of the child's response repertory has evolved from the experimental work of such behavioral scientists

[1] B. F. Skinner. *The behavior of organisms.* New York: Appleton-Century-Crofts, Inc., 1938, p. 20.

as Pavlov, Watson, Thorndike, Skinner, Hull, and Spence, to name only a few.

An important aspect of the child's behavior concerns the stimuli which his own behavior produces and which are capable of influencing his subsequent behavior. The self-produced stimuli come from several sources. Some originate in smooth muscle functioning (the stimulus of bladder pressure leads to releasing of the sphincter muscle), some in fine striped-muscle activity (such as in speech: the stimulus of reminding oneself of the late hour leads to leaving the party), and some in gross striped-muscle movements (such as the regular alternation of leg responses, each stimulated by the other, in pedalling a bicycle). All of the stimuli generated by the child may acquire functional properties relative to the child's own behavior. That is, some may call out certain types of behavior, some may follow the child's responses and strengthen or weaken the preceding behavior, and some may serve as a cue for the child's further behavior. The child, therefore, possesses within himself the capacity to produce stimuli that can affect his behavior, just as do stimuli originating from the external environment.

In summary, the behavior of the developing child is viewed as a cluster of interrelated operant and respondent behaviors, and as a source of stimuli which acquire functional properties in relation to these behaviors. It is assumed that the student understands that the behavior of the child provides social stimulation to other people, and that the larger proportion of the stimuli affecting his behavior originates outside of the body wall. We now turn to a more comprehensive discussion of environmental events.

THE ENVIRONMENT OF DEVELOPMENT

Thus far we have described the environment in terms of specific stimulus events, physical, chemical, organismic, and social. We have also stated that these events may be measured by instruments of physics and chemistry, and/or by changes in behavior produced by the stimuli.

We can explore further the concept of the environment of development (1) by elaborating on the meaning of specific stimulus events, and (2) by introducing a second important category which we shall call *setting events.*[2] We deal with specific stimulus events first by describing the categories of stimuli and citing examples.

1. Physical: man-made and natural things—e.g., eating utensils, tools, tables, chairs, houses, roads, buildings, airplanes, rocks, mountains, trees.
2. Chemical: gases and solutions that act at a distance or on the surface of the skin—e.g., the aroma of roast turkey, perfume, smoke, hydrochloric acid, soap, antiseptic ointment, urine.
3. Organismic: biological structure and physiological functioning of the organism—e.g., stimulation from the respiratory, alimentary, cardiovascular, endocrine, nervous and muscle-skeletal systems of the body.
4. Social: the appearance, action, and interaction of people (and animals)—e.g., mothers, fathers, siblings, teachers, friends, employers, policemen—or of one's self.

Two comments may be appropriate about the way we have classified stimuli. First, it should be made explicit that all stimuli may be analyzed in terms of their physical dimensions. However, we have divided them into convenient subcategories to help the reader understand the range and diversity of stimulation that must be taken into account in analyzing behavior. Second, a stimulus may be measured or detected by the instruments of the physical sciences or by the behavior changes produced by the stimulus in a specified organism. Suppose we invite a five-year-old child into a dimly lighted room (say 50 foot-candles) in which there are a small table and chair. On the table are three attractive toys—an automobile, a doll, and an airplane. We observe the child through a one-way screen for a few minutes

2 J. R. Kantor. *Interbehavioral psychology.* Bloomington: Principia Press, 1958, p. 14.

and then suddenly increase the level of illumination twentyfold. We may describe the abrupt change in the environment (1) by noting the change in the reading of a light meter, and (2) by noting the change in the behavior of the child. If the increase in illumination is consistently correlated with an observable change in the child's behavior, we may state a relationship between the two. Such data would allow us to identify and classify the behavior changes: for example, closing the eyes or leaving the room when the light is bright; or taking the automobile to the light source to examine it when the light is dim. With this kind of information, we can now be more specific about the relationship between the stimulus changes and the behavior changes. We can say that the stimuli stand in a certain functional relationship to the behaviors: the increase in light intensity elicits reflex behavior like a constriction of the child's pupil. When the light is bright, this stimulation sets an occasion on which any response which decreases this stimulation is strengthened (hence eye-closing or leaving the room). When the light is dim, the occasion is set for responses which maximize it (and so the child takes his toy close to the light to look at its details).

When there is a functional relationship between stimulus and response, as in the above examples, we can talk about the *stimulus function* in this relationship. Three kinds of stimulus functions are noted above: an "eliciting" function, a "setting of the occasion" for an appropriate response, and a "strengthening" of that response by its effectiveness in changing the stimulation. Thus, stimulus function is simply a label indicating what the specific action of the stimulus is in the functional relationship being studied. Does it act on the response preceding it, or on a response to follow it? Does it act to strengthen or to weaken a response? Does its action depend on the individual's history with similar stimulation in the past? And so on.

The concept of stimulus function is introduced because it is important to distinguish between stimuli that have functions and stimuli that do not. We may say that a stimulus is any physical, chemical, organismic, or social event that can be measured by us, either directly or by instruments. But not all of these stimuli will have stimulus functions, that is, not all of them will have an effect on behavior. As an example, consider a frown on the face of a parent. For a baby only a few weeks old, we may argue that this could be a stimulus (he can see fairly well at that age), but it probably has no stimulus function: typically, the baby's behavior will not change reliably as a consequence of this stimulation. However, with psychological development, this stimulus will acquire functions: first, like almost any other "face" the parent might make, the parental frown may produce giggles and smiles fairly reliably in the somewhat older infant; later, after the child has some experience with the punishments typically following frowns, it may produce sudden halts in ongoing behavior, sobering, or crying. Hence, the significance of this stimulus lies less in its physical make-up than in its stimulus function.

There is another, and perhaps more important, advantage to concentrating on stimulus functions. If we consider the environment of the developing child in terms of the functions of the stimulus events it contains, we shortcircuit a great deal of cumbersome and fruitless terminology. Stimulus functions concentrate simply and objectively upon the ways in which stimuli control behavior: produce it, strengthen or weaken it, signal occasions for its occurrence or non-occurrence, generalize it to new situations and problems, etc. To understand the psychological development of the child, these are the kinds of actions we need to describe and predict. And stimulus function is precisely the kind of concept which can bring order into the tremendous variety of stimulus events which make up the child's world. In effect, the stimulus function concept is an invitation to group together into a few functional categories many diverse events. A rejecting mother, a spanking, a fall from a bike, a frown, a failing grade, "reasoning" with a misbehaving child, a traffic citation, a snub from an important person—these and many others like them may be regarded as having a common stimulus function; in other words, they are all stimulus events which weaken ("punish") behaviors which produce them. Similarly, a warm mother, a pat on the head, a piece of candy, a ride in the country, a smile, an "A" in psychology, an enthusiastic "Good!", a window sign saying "We Gave," a handshake from the President—these and many others like them may be regarded as having another common stimulus function, that is, they are all stimulus events which may strengthen ("reward") behaviors which produce them. Finally, we should consider such events as a mother's question, "What are you doing?", the sight of a police car, or the announcement of a test next Friday. All such events have the common stimulus function of setting the occasion on which some responses will have stimulus consequences whose function is to strengthen the responses; other responses will have stimulus consequences whose function is to weaken these responses and strengthen others; and still other responses will have stimulus consequences without any function. For example, a mother's question, "What are you doing?" sets an occasion on which the response "Oh, just putting my toys away in their boxes" probably will result in "That's good!" (whose stimulus function is to strengthen responses that produce it). Or the response "Oh, just drawing pictures on the wall" probably will result in a spanking (whose stimulus functions are to weaken responses which produce it and strengthen responses which avoid it—like telling mother a lie instead). Or the response "Oh, nothing" may result in a noncommittal grunt from a busy parent, which may have no stimulus function at all, hence producing no change in behavior.

The classification of environmental events into their stimulus functions provides an organization of the factors that control development and eliminates the need for less objective terms. Child psychology has been burdened with a multitude of terms designed to describe and explain a particular situation in child development. Too often, these terms prove to be non-objective and impossible to apply to behavior in general. Examples may be readily found among the numerous attempts to type parents into largely non-functional categories such as "rejecting," "indulging," "dominating," "democratic," "autocratic," etc. By replacing such schemes with the concept of stimulus function, we concentrate instead upon the kinds of stimuli a parent may provide and their function in strengthening some behaviors of the child, weakening others, and leaving still others unaffected. (We emphasize, however, that these are only some of the possible stimulus functions.) Most of the discussion which follows will be devoted to a description of the stimulus functions important to psychological development.

Now we turn to a consideration of the second category of environmental events—setting events. Setting events, like stimulus events, are environmental changes which affect behavior. But, in contrast to stimulus events, setting events are more complicated than the simple presence, absence, or change of a stimulus (such as turning on a light, a sudden drop in temperature, or a smile from mother). Instead, a setting event is a stimulus-response interaction, which, simply because it has occurred, will affect other stimulus-response relationships which follow it. For example, one mother, who routinely puts her eighteen-month-old son in a playpen after his afternoon nap, has found that during the next hour, the baby will play with his toys, try some gymnastics on the side of the pen, and engage in vigorous vocal play—but he will not fuss (and so mother has free time for an extra cup of coffee and a few telephone calls). However, one day the baby is kept awake during his entire nap time by the unusual and persistent noise of a power mower on the lawn outside his bedroom window. When his mother puts him in the playpen this time, he whimpers, cries, is generally fussy, and does not play.

In this example an analysis of the environment into stimulus events and setting events would proceed this way: First, the playpen is a stimulus event setting the occasion for responses like playing. But this is true only if the child has been previously exposed to the stimulus events of being put to bed and has responded by going to sleep. If, as in the example in the preceding paragraph, the bed-sleep interaction has been prevented (being replaced by the mower-awake interaction), then the child's response to the playpen is no longer playing, but fussing. Thus, the bed-sleep interaction is a necessary setting event for the following playpen-play interaction. In summary, one stimulus-response interaction may be changed because a preceding stimulus-response interaction related to it also has been changed. The preceding interaction is called a setting event.

Clearly enough, we may change some stimulus-response interactions without affecting other subsequent interactions. A child who usually kisses Daddy goodbye as he leaves for work probably will not behave differently if one day Daddy leaves early and thereby precludes the usual affectionate interaction. On the other hand, there are certain interactions which, when changed, typically alter subsequent behaviors of the individual involved. Some of these are changes in the usual sleep cycle or eating cycle; changes in the organism following injury, disease, surgery, or drugs; and any relatively prolonged deprivation of social contact, or, similarly, any current satiation of such stimuli. (Notice how often the loosely used concept of *motivation* can be translated into setting events.) A setting event of particular significance is the use of verbal instructions, such as telling a child "now be a good boy" or "Santa won't bring you any toys unless you behave yourself." These setting events may change his behavior for some time afterwards, especially in that the proportion of "good" behaviors increases and that of "bad" behaviors decreases. Or, a child left with a neighbor may play happily for a few hours if told "Mommy will be back for you soon," but may remain uneasy for a long time if his mother fails to establish this setting event—especially if the child has only a scanty history of being left with neighbors before in his life. In fact, a child's history of past interactions with his environment may be looked upon as a collection of setting events influencing current behavior. A setting event can indeed be analyzed into component stimulus events. It is treated as a separate concept because sometimes it is more convenient and efficient to do so. To sum up, environmental events, made up of specific stimulus events and setting events, function in an interrelated fashion to produce and control psychological behavior.

INTERACTIONS BETWEEN THE DEVELOPING CHILD AND THE ENVIRONMENT

Obviously, stimulus events and setting events interact with the organism's behavior from the moment of fertilization and continue without interruption until death. The fact that interaction is in a sense a continuous flow poses a problem for psychological analysis. Since psychology is concerned with interactions, new and recurrent, between environmental events and responses, present and past, how can the conditions determining an interaction be held constant long enough to allow an investigation to determine what is related to what? The answer is that in experimental studies the concept of continual change is accepted, and arbitrary units of analysis are established in which it is assumed that for the phenomenon studied no significant environmental change is taking place. The interactional unit may be small, requiring only a fraction of a second, or large, covering several months or years, depending on the specific plan of analysis.

In studying the gross influences of past interactions on currently observed behavior, it is convenient to divide the entire developmental interactional stream into stages, and to investigate (1) the interactions within each, and (2) the continuities and discontinuities in behavior between successive units. What is the best way of dividing the developmental cycle? Many have attempted an answer (including Shakespeare, who proposed seven periods or ages). Some psychologists have divided the life span on the basis of chronological age, others on the basis of some personality theory. Age grouping has the virtue of simplicity and objectivity, but is much too arbitrary to be helpful if we are looking for changes within and between successive periods. Interactions resulting in significant behavior changes are not synchronized simply with the ticking of a clock. Basing the initial and terminal points of developmental stages on some personality theory is not fruitful, since at present there is not enough acceptable information on development (i.e., information that is valid and that has been collected in such a way that the data may be systematically related to one another) to allow us to formulate the kind of precise theoretical statements required. In other words, we do not yet have a detailed and comprehensive model of psychological development to serve as a guide for such segmentation. This being the case, we are left with two alternatives. (1) We may mark the beginning and end points of each stage by a mixture of criteria based on environmental events, biological maturational changes, and behavior manifestations. For example, infancy would be the period from birth to the onset of verbal language, childhood the period from entering the first grade in school to the onset of sexual maturity, and adolescence the period from sexual maturity to the age for voting. (2) We may identify the periods in terms of the major types of interactions that take place. We will adopt the second possibility and use the terminology and criteria suggested by Kantor. A brief sketch of the stages is all that is necessary here.

Kantor[3] has suggested that after birth psychological development goes through three major phases—foundational, basic, and societal. The foundational stage starts sometime before birth (at the time the organism is capable of behaving as a unified system) and continues through part of the period commonly called infancy. This period is characterized primarily by respondent (reflex) behavior, by random or uncoordinated movements, and by exploratory (ecological) behavior. The latter, which begins after random movements have become somewhat coordinated, is the first phase of operant behavior. The basic stage starts at the end of infancy and extends into childhood. It may be described as the period in which the contacts with the environment are relatively free from organismic limitations, such as lack of basic equipment, low energy level, need for long hours of sleep or rest, and the like. Interaction during this span builds up repertoires characteristic of the particular individual ("personality"). The societal or cultural period starts when the child begins to have frequent contacts with individuals in groups outside of the family (school, church, neighborhood, etc.) and

[3] J. R. Kantor. *A survey of the science of psychology.* Bloomington: Principia Press, 1933, p. 77.

continues through the adult years. It is identified as consisting of "intimate interpersonal and group conditions."

SUMMARY

The child may be conceptualized as an interrelated cluster of responses and stimuli. The environment is conceived as events acting on the child, some specific stimuli and some setting events. The child and his environment interact continuously from fertilization until death. The psychological development of a child, therefore, is made up of progressive changes in the different ways of interacting with the environment. Progressive development is dependent upon opportunities and circumstances in the present and in the past. The circumstances are physical, chemical, organismic, and social. These influences may be analyzed in their physical and functional dimensions.

Our task now is to describe the specific ways in which behavior (or responses) may be explained as a function of stimulus events, or $B = f(S)$. We shall start with the well-documented observation, mentioned in the section on the developing child, that there are two basic ways in which responses may be related to stimuli: (1) some responses are controlled by *preceding* stimulation; and (2) some responses are controlled by *consequent* stimulation.

1. Respondent
2. Operant

4

Respondent (Reflex) Behavior

ANALYSIS OF PSYCHOLOGICAL INTERACTIONS
INVOLVING RESPONDENTS

The responses in the first class are given the name *respondents* to emphasize the fact that they are responsive to a preceding stimulation.[1] However, it must also be emphasized that this is a particular kind of responsiveness to the preceding stimulus. By this we mean that there is a nearly invariable relationship between stimulus and respondent—whenever the stimulus is presented, the respondent follows it, unless the organism is physically prevented from performing the response, or unless the response systems involved are too fatigued, immature, or injured. We are tempted to believe that the organism is "built that way," that it has no choice in performing the respondent act. Consequently, respondent behavior is often referred to as involuntary behavior.

Respondents are not controlled by their consequences; stimulation which follows them is not liable to affect them. For example, reduction in size of the pupil of the eye is a respondent. This response is elicited by presenting a bright light to the open-eyed organism, and the contracting response invariably follows. You may stand in front of a mirror with a flashlight and observe the changes in size of your own pupils. If you try it, try also to prevent the response as you turn the flashlight to shine in your eye: "will yourself" not to contract your pupil. You will fail to

[1] B. F. Skinner. *The behavior of organisms.* New York: Appleton-Century-Crofts, Inc., 1938, p. 20.

prevent the response. Similarly, someone might stand beside you and offer you $100 if you will *not* contract your pupil as the light is shined in. You will still fail to prevent the response when the eliciting stimulus is applied. Again, someone might tell you that he will give you $100 if you *will* contract the pupil of your eye. Unless you can arrange for an eliciting stimulus of a light to flash in your eye, you will fail to win the $100.[2] Respondents, therefore, are simply functions of the particular kinds of stimulation which precede them, not functions of stimulations which follow them.

THE ATTACHMENT OF RESPONDENT BEHAVIOR TO NEW STIMULI

Let us consider as an example the blushing that is elicited by "shameful" situations. Blushing is a surface manifestation of a biological response, the dilation of the blood vessels in the face. This is one of a set of responses the human is liable to show when he is excited. One reason for becoming excited might be punishment. A child, when punished, typically blushes (and cries, and displays many other responses, too). A child may well be punished in situations which his parents define as "shameful" (i.e., worthy of punishment). And subsequently we observe that the child, even in his adult years, may blush when something reminds him of the punishment or when he is in a similarly "shameful" situation. Yet he is not necessarily being punished on these occasions.

An analysis would proceed along these lines: blushing is one of a number of respondents elicited by punishment. Some of the characteristics of any stimulus situation which also includes punishment apparently come to elicit blushing, just as punishment does, simply because they have been associated with punishment in the child's experience. For example, a young child may

2 On pages 81–82 we will list some techniques which would allow you to win this bet. However, as you will have seen by then, this possibility does not abridge the statements made here about the insensitivity of respondent behaviors to their stimulus consequences.

be punished by his parents for being naked, past a certain age of tolerance. In particular, the parents are liable to punish a boy for exposing his genitals in public. Thus, they associate a certain culturally defined situation, exposure of the genitals, with a certain biologically powerful stimulus, physical punishment, which (among other things) elicits blushing. Later in life, the man may discover that he has been walking about with his trousers unzipped. He is very liable to blush. He has not been presented with punishment; he has been presented with a stimulus associated with punishment in his past history. Clearly, this is a *conditioned* power. Without his particular history of punishment for this kind of exposure, the discovery that his pants have been open for some time would not elicit blushing.

Similarly, food placed in our mouths usually elicits salivation, another example of a respondent. It is because the sight of food is almost invariably associated with the stimulus of food in the mouth that the sight of food develops eliciting power for salivation. Were we invariably blindfolded before we eat, the sight of food no doubt would not elicit salivation for us; it would have then no history of association with the naturally effective eliciting stimulus of food in the mouth.

We may sum up the basic principles of this discussion in the general formula of respondent conditioning:

A stimulus which initially has no power to elicit a respondent may come to have such power, if it is consistently associated with a stimulus which does have the power to elicit the respondent.

This formula is an old one in psychology, dating back to Pavlov[3] as a formal principle of conditioning. It has been given a number of names since then, any of which you may meet in other readings in psychology. Examples are Pavlovian conditioning, classical conditioning, stimulus substitution, associative shifting, and type S conditioning (S emphasizing the importance of the stimulus in its eliciting function). Respondents, as you probably have

[3] I. P. Pavlov. *Conditioned reflexes.* London: Oxford University Press, 1927.

gathered from the examples given, are largely restricted to those behaviors popularly called "reflexes" and "emotional behavior." (We prefer Skinner's technical usage of "respondent" to these popular terms since we can state with precision what we mean by "respondent," but would have considerable trouble sharpening the popular meaning of "reflex" or "emotion.") Hence respondent conditioning, as a form of learning, is also restricted to these behaviors.

Two points must be understood about respondent conditioning. First, it should be noted that no new response is created in the conditioning process. Some of the features of the response, such as its amplitude or duration, may be altered, but basically it is the same response that is called out by its appropriate eliciting stimulus. The second point is that not all respondents are conditionable. A tap on the patellar tendon accompanied by an audible tone has never, no matter how often the paired stimuli are repeated, produced the knee jerk in response to the tone alone. Respondents of this type will not be included in this discussion. They may be thought of as organismic phenomena, as neurological reflexes, the kind of responses the neurologist seeks out by tapping you in strategic spots with a little rubber-headed hammer.

THE DETACHMENT OF RESPONDENT BEHAVIOR
FROM CONDITIONED STIMULI

What we have said is this: a stimulus which has been demonstrated to lack power to elicit a respondent may be given such power by pairing it with an eliciting stimulus. Now, the power so acquired may be weakened or eliminated by simply stopping the pairing, by repeatedly presenting the conditioned stimulus without the eliciting stimulus. When the conditioned stimulus is repeatedly presented alone, the respondent will be elicited at first, but finally it will disappear, so that the conditioned stimulus reverts to its original neutral state with respect to the respondent. We say that the conditioned respondent has now been *extinguished,* or deconditioned, or that the stimuli that were con·

ditioned to bring it forth have been detached. For example, Watson and Raynor[4] conditioned respondent crying in a nine-month-old infant by using the sight of a rat as the conditioned eliciting stimulus. Their method was to pair the sight of the rat (which originally did not elicit crying in the infant) with a loud, sudden noise, which did elicit strong crying. After only five pairings of sight of the rat and the loud noise (produced by striking a steel bar with a hammer), the presentation of the rat alone was sufficient to elicit crying in the child. Later, though, after the rat had been presented alone repeatedly, the crying response grew successively weaker, its strength approaching closer to zero with each repeated exposure of the rat alone.

Mary Cover Jones[5] varied this method so as to accelerate the detachment of a respondent from a conditioned eliciting stimulus. Working under Watson's direction with another child who already had been conditioned to cry at the sight of a rabbit (repeated presentation of the rabbit without any other stimulus eliciting crying), she associated the sight of the rabbit with occasions on which the child was eating candy. This hastened the course of extinction, that is, crying was detached from the stimulus of the rabbit more quickly this way than by merely showing the rabbit alone.

GENERALIZATION AND DISCRIMINATION OF RESPONDENT BEHAVIOR

It is a fact of casual observation as well as repeated laboratory demonstrations that conditioned respondents may be elicited by stimuli other than those specifically involved in the conditioning process. Recall the previous example of how Watson and Raynor[6] taught a nine-month-old baby to fear a white rat by accompanying its appearance with the loud sound. This sound typically

---

[4] J. B. Watson and Rosalie A. Raynor. Conditioned emotional reactions. *J. exp. Psychol.*, 1920, 3, 1-4.

[5] Mary C. Jones. A laboratory study of fear: the case of Peter. *Pedagogical Seminary*, 1924, 31, 308-315.

[6] Watson and Raynor, *op. cit.*

elicits from an infant the unconditioned respondent of crying. The child's response to the rat prior to the pairing was positive, consisting of approaching and reaching responses. (Children do not fear rats unless they are taught to.) But after five pairings his responses to the rat presented alone changed to crying. This is simply a demonstration of respondent conditioning involving the same conditioned stimulus, the rat. Now the investigators presented to the child, in succession, a rabbit, a dog, a sealskin coat, and a mass of white cotton. These objects were not previously paired with the loud noise, nor did they previously elicit crying. But they are all furry, white, or both, and now they all elicited crying. Elicitation of a respondent by stimuli which are merely like the one involved in the original pairing is termed respondent stimulus generalization. Research has demonstrated that the greater the resemblance, the stronger the conditioned reaction.

In the same study, the investigators presented the baby with a set of wooden blocks. The baby did not cry; instead, he showed his usual manipulative behavior toward blocks. On the basis of the difference in behavior in the two situations we may say that the youngster formed a *discrimination*. That is, he responded to objects resembling the rat by crying, and to things not white and not furry in texture (like blocks) with other behaviors. The investigators could have taught the child to make discriminations even among the objects that showed generalized respondent crying. To do this they would have continued to pair rats and loud noise, and at the same time presented one of the other objects, say the mass of white cotton, without the loud noise. After enough contrasts, the child would be expected to continue to show respondent reactions to the rat, but not to the cotton. When this had occurred, we would say that the child had learned a *respondent discrimination*, that is, a previously generalized conditioned reaction was gone, replaced by other responses, such as looking, touching, and babbling. Many of these reactions are not even respondents, as we shall now see.

5

Operant Behavior

ANALYSIS OF PSYCHOLOGICAL INTERACTIONS INVOLVING OPERANTS

The second basic way in which responses are a function of stimuli involves the stimulus *consequences* of responding, or the changes the response causes in the stimulus world. Behaviors which are best understood as functionally related to their consequences in the environment are called *operants*. The word "operant" is used because it suggests that the individual operates upon his environment (which includes his own body) to produce some stimulus event or change in a stimulus event or setting event. Some examples are turning on the TV set, which results in picture and sound; asking a friend for the time, which produces "It's two o'clock"; building a fire on a camping trip, which is followed by warmth; and removing a cinder from your eye, which relieves the irritation. Operant behavior is involved in "trial-and-error" behavior, and the response that is the solution to such a sequence is strengthened by the "reward." Furthermore, most of the fields of behavior designated by Gesell and Ilg[1] as motor, adaptive, language, and personal-social are operants. This broad class of responses is for the most part actions of striped muscles, and is sometimes called voluntary behavior. Such a label is acceptable and even helpful in understanding psychological development, provided there is no added implica-

[1] Arnold Gesell and Frances L. Ilg. *Child development.* New York: Harper, 1949.

tion of the "will," "awareness," "consciousness," or "understanding."

The fact that the strength of operant behavior is dependent
upon its past effects on the environment has been widely recognized. Note the many descriptive statements in psychology that
behavior is "goal-directed," "purposeful," or "instrumental" in
achieving the organism's ends; behavior is "adient" (directed
toward certain consequences) or "abient" (directed away from
certain consequences); behavior is "wish-fulfilling," or "pleasure-
seeking" and "pain-avoiding." All of these phrases emphasize the
results of behavior as the essential factor which makes sense to
the observer. However, such expressions may also imply that the
child actively seeks or desires certain stimuli, and that he chooses
certain behaviors because they are likely to achieve these goals.
We wish to avoid such implications. We do this by simply stating
*that operants are controlled by stimulus consequences, those
observed in the child's current situation as well as those in his
past history.*

Operants may produce consequences in the following ways:

1. They may produce certain stimulus events and as a result
   the operants increase in frequency. These stimuli are called
   positive reinforcers.
2. They may remove, avoid, or terminate certain other stimulus
   events and as a result the operants increase in frequency.
   These stimuli are called *negative reinforcers.*
3. They may produce *or* remove still other stimuli which fit
   neither of these categories, that is, which fail to strengthen
   a response, whether the response produces the stimulus or
   removes it. These stimuli are called *neutral stimuli.*

The first group, stimuli which strengthen the behavior they
follow, are called positive because they involve an *adding* operation, and reinforcing because the behavior producing the stimulus is strengthened. Some examples are milk (especially for a
baby), candy (especially for a toddler), the approval of parents
(especially for a young school child), the esteem of peers (es-

pecially for a teenager), and dollars received from an employer (especially for a young adult). The second class, stimuli which tend to strengthen responses that remove, avoid, or terminate them, are called negative because they involve a *subtracting* operation, and reinforcing because the behavior causing this removal is strengthened. Some examples are cold air (especially for an infant), a spanking (especially for a toddler), a frown from mother (especially for the young child), the ridicule of peers (especially for the teenager), and a ticket from a traffic cop (especially for the young adult). The third class of stimuli, those which do not affect the strength of responses they follow or are removed by, are neutral in that *neither an adding nor a subtracting operation* changes the strength of the operant from its usual level. Some examples are the parents' frown for the new baby, or the seductive overture of an attractive young lady for a typical ten-year-old boy. (In general, the older the child, the harder it is to find stimuli which are neutral for him. The reason for this will become apparent soon.)

How can we tell whether a particular stimulus (e.g., movement of the teacher's head in the direction of a child in her classroom, offering a piece of graham cracker to a preschool child, placing a young child in a room alone, offering a ride on a bike, saying "Is that so?") will be a positive reinforcer, a negative reinforcer, or a neutral stimulus for a given child? We cannot tell[2] unless we make the following test. We observe some response which is clearly an operant, and which has a stable strength for a child (occurs fairly frequently on prescribed occasions). Then we arrange conditions so that the stimulus to be evaluated as a reinforcer is consistently presented to the child as a consequence of that response. (For example, each time the child says "Mar-

[2] In many instances we are able to make a good guess because of what we know about the culture that the child shares. For example, we know that in our culture saying, "That's fine" when a child completes a performance will for *most* children strengthen the tendency to repeat that act under similar circumstances. However, we know, too, that it would be wrong to assume that saying, "That's fine" will strengthen the preceding behavior for *all* children, and indeed, we may know some "negativistic" children for whom "That's fine" seems to be a negative reinforcer.

mar," the thing or event, say a marble, is immediately given.)
If the response increases in strength (e.g., saying "Mar-mar"
occurs more often), the marble may be classified as a positive
reinforcer. The observation of this relationship defines the stimulus as a positive reinforcer; no other kind of observation or judg-
ment is necessary or sufficient. By the same token, we may
arrange the situation so that the operant to be observed removes
or avoids a stimulus. If the response is strengthened under these
conditions, that observation alone is necessary and sufficient to
classify the stimulus as a negative reinforcer. Finally, if the
operant in either of these tests remains unaffected in strength,
continuing at the usual stable level of strength it showed before
the test, then the stimulus is classified as neutral.

We have been talking about the *strength* of a response. Let
us clarify the meaning of the term. In psychological work, as in
everyday conversation, we measure or estimate the strength of
a response in several ways. During the past thirty years it has
been demonstrated that one of the most useful criteria for psychology is the *rate* of response: how often it occurs in a unit of
time under a given set of conditions. The frequency with which
a response occurs is one of the most common questions raised
in evaluating the behavior of a child, for example, "How often
does he suck his thumb?" A second measure of the strength of
a response is the *magnitude* (or *amplitude*) *of the response*, or
the effort invested in it, or the vigor with which it is performed.
A child may whisper, remark, or shout "Go away," as increasing
evidence of his anti-social behavior. A third measure of response strength is its *latency*, or the promptness with which it is
emitted in reference to a stimulus. The child who responds to a
gift with a prompt "Thank you" is considered more polite than
one who makes the same response sometime later. When psychologists talk about response strength, they may be referring to
any of these measures or to some combination of them. It is
important to be aware of the dimension used, for they are not
always equivalent. Two studies dealing with some aspect of the
relationship between, say, aggression and hunger may result in

different conclusions if one investigator measures the strength of aggressive behavior by frequency of occurrence, and the other by magnitude. Unless otherwise stated, when we talk about the strength of an operant, we shall be referring to the *rate* of responding.

We have pointed out that a response may result in the presentation of the stimulus, or in the removal, avoidance, or turning-off of the stimulus. We have also suggested that the two kinds of stimulus consequences which affect the strength of the response may be called positive and negative reinforcers. Keeping this terminology in mind and disregarding the effect of neutral stimuli for the moment, we can see that an operant may have four kinds of consequences:

1. Produce positive reinforcers.
2. Remove or avoid negative reinforcers.
3. Produce negative reinforcers.
4. Remove or avoid positive reinforcers.

When the first procedure results in an increase in response strength, we know the stimulus to be a positive reinforcer, by definition; when the second procedure results in an increase in response strength, we know the stimulus to be a negative reinforcer, by definition. What will be the effect under conditions three and four? Repeated observations in experimentally controlled situations, with both animals and humans, give a consistent answer: in each case the net effect is to weaken the response. Thus, at this point, we have two techniques for strengthening responses and two for weakening responses. It will be recalled that the strengthening of a response is measured by an increase in its rate, an increase in its magnitude, or a decrease in its latency. Thus, the weakening of a response is seen in a decrease in its rate, a decrease in its magnitude, or an increase in its latency. The relationships among the ways operants affect the environment, and the effects of these stimulus consequences on the operant, may be summed up in the following four-fold table.

TABLE I

Results of Interactions between Operants and the
Stimulus Environment

Effect of the operant on the stimulus environment	Effect of the stimulus function on the operant	Classification of the stimulus (i.e., the stimulus function)
Produces stimulus	Strengthened ("reward")	Positive reinforcer
	weakened ("punishment by hurt")	Negative reinforcer
Removes or avoids stimulus	weakened ("punishment by loss")	Positive reinforcer
	Strengthened ("relief")	Negative reinforcer

In the cells of column 2 of Table I we have listed some popular terms whose meanings often coincide with the much more precise meanings these procedures now have for psychology. They are included only to help you understand the theory. They are not used throughout the text because they often imply more than we wish. "Reward" in particular may be misleading. It often suggests a flavor of conscious wishing for the reinforcer on the part of the child, a deliberate choosing of his responses in a judicious, rational manner, so that these responses seem likely to achieve the reinforcer. If this were the case, it would be reasonable to call the reinforcer a "goal," the operant response "purposeful," and the reinforcer a "reward." But we have no way of knowing whether this is so. Remember that we must use these terms to explain the developing behavior of the human child, from birth onward. It would not be appropriate to apply to a newborn infant, squalling helplessly in his crib, terms which might suggest that he is consciously desiring certain goals and deliberately computing ways and means of achieving them. We will be closer to empirical facts (and further from mentalistic explanations) if we simply say, for example, "Since milk has been tested and found to be a positive reinforcer, operant responses by the infant which result in milk will therefore tend to be strengthened, whereas operant responses which remove or lose milk will tend to be weakened." (And *this* summary of empirical relationships between certain responses and stimuli provides a good example of what we mean by a "theoretical" statement.)

We have now described the basic formulae of *operant control* by giving the essential characteristics of operant responses and the four ways in which operants may be changed in strength. All of these we might call examples of operant *conditioning,* that is, of ways of changing the strength of a response using reinforcers as consequences of that response. However, the term conditioning is often restricted to those operations that *strengthen* responses. Let us instead call each of these four basic procedures a "reinforcement" procedure. Furthermore, we shall say that these four reinforcement procedures completely define the basic ways in which an operant may be controlled by reinforcing consequences, and that all other procedures involved in the reinforcement of operant responses are variations or combinations of these four.

THE WEAKENING OF OPERANTS THROUGH NEUTRAL STIMULUS CONSEQUENCES

Now let us return to a consideration of the effects of neutral stimuli as a consequence of operant behavior. Once a response has been strengthened through reinforcement, what will happen when reinforcement ceases, that is, when the only consequences of a response are neutral stimuli? We have already defined a neutral stimulus as one which will fail to strengthen a response of which it is a consequence. But what if that response has been built up to considerable strength through reinforcing consequences, and then circumstances change so that the only results of the response are neutral stimuli?

A partial answer is that the response eventually will weaken.

In fact, it will weaken until its strength is equal to that shown before it was strengthened through reinforcement. The degree of strength characterizing a response *before* it is affected by reinforcement is called its *operant level*. (Note that a response cannot have a zero operant level, or it could never be reinforced.) The weakening of a response by consistently giving it only neutral stimulus consequences, until it falls in strength to its operant level, is called *extinction* of the response. When the response has fallen to its operant level and stabilized at that strength, it is said to be *extinguished*.

This is only a partial answer to the question of what happens when a response is no longer reinforced. Other behaviors show changes, too. Some of these are respondents of a kind we call "emotional" (e.g., frustration); some are operants which in the past may also have been successful in producing the same reinforcement ("He's trying to figure out what went wrong").

Extinction obviously is similar to punishment in that its effect is to weaken the response to which it is applied. Hence, there are three procedures which weaken responses:

1. Response produces a negative reinforcer (punishment).
2. Response loses a positive reinforcer (punishment).
3. Response produces a neutral stimulus (extinction).

However, these three procedures differ in certain essential respects. Extinction weakens a response so that it eventually falls to operant level. The two punishment procedures *may* be used so effectively that they weaken a response well below its operant level. This raises a question parallel to the one which introduced this section: What happens to a response, strengthened through reinforcement, when it produces only neutral stimuli? Similarly, it may be asked, what happens to a response *weakened* through *punishment*, when it produces only neutral stimuli? In general, the answer is that it will rise in strength to its pre-punishment level, or its operant level. This process is sometimes called "recovery."

Thus, a neutral stimulus may be redefined in terms of operant level: a neutral stimulus is one which, whether produced or removed by a response, will fail to change the response from operant level or to maintain it above or below operant level.

For an example, let us imagine a toddler slightly over one year of age, just learning to make a few recognizable verbal responses which its fond parents are more than willing to recognize as words. The toddler's mother, we shall say, is fond of giving him sugar cookies, and usually says to the youngster, "Here's your cookie" when she hands him one. Now, if we were to examine the verbal responses of the child, we might find quite a number of syllabic responses, not otherwise recognizable as English words. One such response might be "Doo doo." This is a verbal sound, we find, which this child makes about once or twice a day (its operant level). In general, it is received by the parents rather absent-mindedly, and, having no other stimulus consequences which are reinforcing, this response remains at its operant level. However, one day the mother happens to hear the child saying "Doo doo," and for reasons of her own, decides that the child is asking her for a cookie. With good will and warmth, she rushes to get the child a cookie, which she presents, saying, "Here's your Doo doo!" After this, whenever she hears her child saying "Doo doo," she gives it a cookie together with a smile plus some obvious delight. Now, we discover the strength of "Doo doo" is increasing: the child says it ten or twelve times a day, and increasingly, on the occasions when he uses it, keeps using it until it results in cookie-plus-smile-plus-delight, so that more and more often we find him saying not simply "Doo doo," but "Doo doo, doo doo, doo doo, . ." From these observations, it is clear that the response is being reinforced, perhaps by the cookie, or by mother's smile, or by her delight, or by all three. Thus we have an example of operant conditioning through the presentation of positive reinforcement for a particular response, "Doo doo."

But now the situation changes. Mother reads in the Sunday paper that some famous dentist believes that too much sugar will promote tooth decay, especially in very young children. She is horrified to think that her practice of giving her child sugar cookies may be melting his teeth. The next time the child says "Doo doo," the mother neither smiles nor shows delight, nor does she give the child a cookie. And from that point on, "Doo doo" is followed by only neutral stimulation, as it was before the mother decided it meant "cookie." We shall probably observe that the child continues to say "Doo doo" for some time, but as occasion follows occasion when the response has been emitted and followed only by neutral stimulation, we shall see its strength falling until the response is back at operant level. That is, once again the child is saying "Doo doo" only once or twice a day. And so we have an example of operant extinction.

But, you may say, this is too pat—the chances are that when the child asks for cookies the mother will not withhold her smiles, delights and cookies, but rather will tell the child that cookies are not good for him, will console him, and may even suggest another activity "to distract him." This may indeed happen. If it does, it is highly probable that the response of "Doo doo" will take longer to weaken since mother is reinforcing "Doo doo" with her attention, affection, or other social reinforcers.

There are several other points about operant conditioning to be gleaned from this example. For instance, it might be asked, "Which of the three obvious stimulus consequences of this response reinforced it?" We do not know, but we could find out by applying the definition of positive reinforcer to each. Mother might continue giving a cookie for the response, but stop smiling and showing delight. If the strength of the response is unaffected, we might conclude that the cookie was the critical reinforcement. But we should also have the mother stop giving the cookie, but continue to smile for the response, while withholding all signs of delight. And we should also have the mother continue to show delight, but withhold smiling and/or giving cookies. We might discover that any of these stimuli is effective in continuing "Doo doo" at its high frequency, or that one is more effective than another, or that two in combination are more than twice as effective as either alone. The essential point here is a reiteration of what has been said about reinforcers: you can tell only by testing. It is worth emphasizing again that because of differences in individual histories and the current stimulus situation, one child may be better reinforced by cookies, another better reinforced by mother's smile, and a third better reinforced by her delight. There are relatively few reinforcers that will work for everybody; each child may be reinforceable by a different list of stimuli. We can only make such a list by testing stimuli that vary over a wide range. And, indeed, we submit that one of the most basic ways of accounting for the wide differences in personality that distinguish children is to list and rank in order the important reinforcers for each individual child.

A second point to note in the example is that *no new response was created by the reinforcement procedure*. An already existing response was strengthened. A response can be conditioned by reinforcing consequences *but it must occur in order to have consequences*. In operant conditioning we do not produce new responses; instead, we strengthen or weaken old ones, and put them together in new combinations. For example, we may take a young child who does not play the piano, and after a few years of proper reinforcement produce reasonably creditable playing. We have not strengthened "piano playing" from zero strength to a considerable positive value. Instead, we have separately reinforced a large number of already existing finger movement responses, strung them together in novel combinations, and established some standard time intervals between them (rhythm), through a long and complex series of strengthening (and weakening) procedures. Then we have labeled this chain of responses "piano playing" as if it were a new response, but it is in fact the arrangement which is new, not the responses that go into it.

If operant conditioning does not create new responses, but instead merely strengthens, weakens, and rearranges old ones, then where do the old responses come from? The answer lies with the biologist, since this question has to do with the make-up, equipment, and biological functioning of the human organism. It will be recalled that in the introductory section, in discussing the relationship between animal biology and psychology, it was stated that psychology looks to biology for information about the equipment of the organism at various times in the developmental cycle. Psychologists accept from biologists the fact that these responses *do* exist, and study them as they interact with environmental events. Similarly, astronomers account for the behavior of stars but not for the *facts* of stars, chemists for the behavior of elements but not for the elements themselves.

A third point to be stressed in this example concerns interpreting the meaning that "Doo doo" may have for the child. All that is known to the observer is that "Doo doo" is a verbal response which is reinforced by cookies. It does not follow that the child will name cookies "Doo doo" when he sees them, nor does it follow that the child will think of cookies when he hears someone else say "Doo doo." It would even be stretching a point to say that the child "wants" cookies when he makes this response. In general, we cannot attribute any other significance to the response for this child. Our example gives us no special insights into such concepts as the child's inner mental world.

Now we turn to some basic principles of operant behavior which refine and supplement those already discussed.

TEMPORAL RELATIONS BETWEEN OPERANTS AND REINFORCEMENTS

We have emphasized that operants are sensitive to their consequences. The *promptness* with which an operant has consequences can be as important as the consequences themselves. Investigations have shown that the more immediately a response is reinforced, the more effectively will its strength be changed by that reinforcement. In technical terms we refer to this relationship as the *temporal gradient of reinforcement*. To exemplify this gradient, imagine Father coming home one night, tired from a hard day's work, and sinking into his favorite armchair with the newspaper before supper. Mother, observing the general state of fatigue of her spouse, calls their two-year-old aside and says, "Bring Daddy his slippers." Assuming that this is an intelligible suggestion to the child, he may comply to please mother. The moment the youngster approaches Father with the slippers is critical. If Father immediately looks up from his paper, sees the child arriving with the slippers, and bursts out in a delighted "Well! What have we here?", then the slipper-carrying response may be greatly strengthened by this prompt reinforcement (if Father's delight is a good reinforcing stimulus for this child). As a consequence, it is probable that the next time the same act is appropriate (the next evening when Father again sinks into his chair to read his paper), the child will again bring his slippers, perhaps without a suggestion from mother. If, again, Father is punctual with his reinforcement, the response will be further strengthened, and will be well on its way toward becoming one of the household rituals.

Now consider the consequence of another course of action. Suppose that on that first occasion, the child brought the slippers, but found Father so deeply engrossed in the funnies that he did not notice the arrival of his slippers. Perhaps he would discover them several minutes later, and say something about being delighted, but by then the child might be playing with blocks in the middle of the floor. According to the temporal gradient of reinforcement, the response which profits most by Father's reinforcement will be what the child is doing at the instant of the reinforcement, and now it is block-stacking, not slipper-bringing. From the point of view of wanting to strengthen slipper-fetching, we are off to a bad start. The child is not likely to repeat the slipper-bringing response the next time it may be proper to do so, unless Mother again suggests to the child that he should. And if she does, Father had better be more prompt with his reinforcement, or the act may never become habitual.

Some of the observations psychologists have made on the effectiveness of prompt reinforcement illustrate the basic nature of the rule, "What is learned is what is reinforced." Skinner[3] has taught pigeons to peck at a disc on the wall of a cage by reinforcing this response with a buzzing sound (which is reinforcing

---

[3] B. F. Skinner. *Cumulative record.* New York: Appleton-Century-Crofts, Inc., 1959, p. 133.

to the pigeon because it has been associated with food—a principle we shall discuss presently). He has shown that if the buzzer is presented even *one-twentieth of a second* after the pigeon has pecked at the disc, the pecking response will not be learned easily. Amazing? Let's see why this is so. When a pigeon pecks at a disc, the sequence of responses are very swift and precise, so precise that when a reinforcement arrives more than one-twentieth of a second after the pigeon's bill hits the disc, it is a closer consequence of the recoil of the pigeon's head from the disc than of the approach of the head towards the disc. Hence the backward motion of the head is reinforced more promptly than the forward motion of the head, and what the pigeon begins to learn is to jerk his head *backward*. One might think that a bright pigeon would "see" what was involved in getting the reinforcement, and would peck the disc accordingly. But investigations of learning seem more and more to show that it is less important what an organism can "deduce" from a set of experiences than what response was most promptly reinforced. A question to keep in mind from this point forward might be: How much of child development can we explain by using the systematic principles described here, while completely ignoring ideas of what a child ought to be able to "figure out," "deduce," "see," "know," or "understand?"

NUMBER OF REINFORCEMENTS AND STRENGTH OF AN OPERANT

Our last example stressing the significance of the time between the response and its reinforcement should raise this question: Since people can hardly reinforce other people within a fraction of a second of the response, how do children ever learn anything?

The temporal gradient of reinforcement is an important principle: but equally important is another principle, which explains why the relatively slow and imprecise reinforcement practices of parents, teachers, and peers succeed in developing the children's behavior. This principle may be stated as follows: the strength of an operant depends upon the number of times it has been reinforced in the past. The more often it has produced positive reinforcers or the removal of negative reinforcers, the stronger it becomes within limits; the more often it has produced negative reinforcers, neutral stimuli, or the removal of positive reinforcers, the weaker it becomes.

Let us re-examine the example of the pigeon in the light of both the temporal gradient of reinforcement and the number of reinforcements. Every time the pigeon pecks at the disc, he emits two responses, "head-forward," followed by "head-back." If the reinforcement (the sound of the buzzer) arrives more than a twentieth of a second late, it follows both of these responses, and thus both are reinforced an equal *number* of times, but the "head-back" response is strengthened more than the "head-forward" response (since it is more promptly reinforced), and as a result the pigeon does not learn to peck properly at the disc. We may apply the same two principles to the child who brings Father his slippers. The child may learn slowly because Father cannot apply his reinforcement (delight) as quickly as a mechanical instrument might reinforce a pigeon. And any response which happens to intervene between the arrival of the child with the slippers and Father's reinforcement will profit more from the reinforcement than will the slipper-bringing response. But in this example, we can see that the responses which intervene between slipper-bringing and reinforcement are liable to be different ones each time the child approaches Father: perhaps he will stand and look at Father, perhaps he will look at the slippers, perhaps he will say something, or perhaps he will pet the dog who happens by at that instant. In other words, we would expect a reasonably random sample of behaviors to occur between the time the child arrives and the time Father gives the reinforcement. In terms of the distribution of reinforcements, then, we see that it is the slipper-bringing response which is reinforced every time, however belatedly, while the other responses are (each) reinforced perhaps more immediately but usually less often. Thus, if Father is not *too* slow in applying reinforcement, slipper-bringing eventually will be strengthened more than the other responses since it is more consistently reinforced, and it will be learned. The quicker Father is, the quicker will the youngster learn to bring his slippers. But if father is *too* slow, the gradient of reinforcement may not allow any learning at all, even though the *consistently* reinforced response is slipper-bringing.

Much of the young child's learning may be characterized by the operation of these two principles, the temporal gradient of reinforcement and the number of reinforcements. Learning will typically be slow, because of the slow and imprecise reinforcement practices of the parents and teachers. Frequently, learning may not take place at all simply because the reinforcement is too slow, so that the intervening responses manage to be better reinforced. But often enough the child will learn (obviously, he does), probably because, imprecise as their reinforcements may be, parents and teachers are at least reasonably consistent and persistent in recognizing the particular behavior they wish to reinforce.

Before concluding the discussion of the number of reinforcements and strength of an operant, two other cardinal points must be made. The first is that it is possible for a response to be considerably strengthened as a consequence of a single reinforcement. In general we would expect such a strengthening to take place if the interval between response and reinforcement were very small, if the reinforcers were very powerful (e.g., food after prolonged fasting or a strong electric shock delivered to the feet), if the response itself were a simple one, and if it had already been considerably strengthened in some other similar situation.

The second point is that we are talking about the number of reinforcements, not the number of responses. The number of responses by itself does not tell us much about what to expect concerning the strength of learning. Investigations have repeatedly shown that the mere repetition of a response is not automatically strengthening, and hence that practice does not make perfect unless each response leads to reinforcement or contributes to a sequence of responses which leads to reinforcement.

These findings deserve very careful consideration for they have far-reaching implications, both practical and theoretical.

GENERALIZATION AND DISCRIMINATION OF OPERANT BEHAVIOR

This topic might be best introduced with a few examples. A preadolescent boy may observe the frown on his father's face and hear his irritated voice commenting on the lateness of supper, and decide not to ask for an advance on his allowance. The frown and the voice are stimuli marking an occasion in which the operant response of requesting more allowance will probably fail to be reinforced: Father will refuse. Later, though, observing Father enjoying his favorite magazine, puffing away on his pipe, with his feet up, the boy may make the request with a higher probability of success, that is, of having the response reinforced with money. Another example: a red traffic light is a stimulus marking an occasion when crossing the street may be negatively reinforced, either by being knocked down by a car or being cited by a policeman. A green light, however, marks an occasion when crossing the street will avoid these negative reinforcers, and get us farther on our way toward other reinforcers. Another: the ringing of an alarm clock is a stimulus signalling a time when we must either arise or suffer the negative reinforcement of being late to class or to work. Again: Friday is a stimulus, as well as a day, and for many people it marks a time when going to work will be reinforced with the weekly paycheck. And for many people, it also marks a time which will not be followed (on Saturday) by the negative reinforcers involved in their week-day jobs. Friday night often signals a time when the alarm clock need not be set.

Thus we see that there are many stimuli which *precede* and control our behaviors, not because they elicit respondents, but because they promise various types of reinforcements as consequences of certain operants. Let us give such stimuli a name: any stimulus which marks a time or place of reinforcement, positive or negative, being presented or removed, is known as a *discriminative stimulus.*

At this point the reader should recall the previous insistence that operants are controlled by their stimulus consequences, whereas respondents are controlled by their stimulus antecedents. Now we may seem to be blurring this clear distinction by saying that operants are controlled by preceding *as well as* by consequent stimulation. The distinction still holds, however, because its crucial feature remains unchanged—a preceding discriminative stimulus can control an operant only because it marks a time or place when that operant will have reinforcing consequences. The important characteristic of operants is still their sensitivity to stimulus consequences; therefore, preceding stimuli may control operants only because they are cues to the nature of this important consequent stimulation. The term *cue* is sometimes used to designate a stimulus having discriminative properties.[4]

It is important to understand at this point that a discriminative stimulus *does not elicit responses.* Elicitation is a characteristic that holds only for respondents. The green traffic light does not set us going across the street in the same way that a bright light flashed in our eyes constricts our pupils. The pupillary response is controlled by the bright light, quite independent of its consequences; crossing the street is controlled by the green light because of the special consequences of crossing the street at that time, as opposed to other (red light) times, and because of our history of reinforcement and extinction in relation to green, amber, and red traffic lights.

Now, whenever we see a person consistently emitting a certain operant response in close conjunction with some discriminative stimulus which marks a reinforcement occasion, let us call that response a *discriminated operant,* that is, one controlled by a preceding discriminative stimulus. A person who typically responds under the control of discriminative stimuli is said to be discriminating; the procedure of bringing an operant under such

4 John Dollard and N. R. Miller. *Personality and psychotherapy.* New York: McGraw-Hill, 1950, p. 32.

control is called discrimination. This process has crucial significance for developmental psychology. Consider that the infant is
born into a world, ready to be reinforced by a number of stimuli
(milk, temperature, sleep, oxygen, open diaper pins, ammonia,
etc.), but thoroughly unacquainted with the stimuli which signal
the occasions when these reinforcers are experienced. A great
part of psychological development, therefore, is simply the
process of learning the discriminative stimuli which signal important reinforcements. Mother, for example, is a discriminative
stimulus for many reinforcers: she brings baby milk, adjusts the
temperature with sweaters and blankets, rocks the child to sleep,
rescues him from open pins, changes his wet, irritating diapers,
and so forth. Later in life, the child may learn that Mother's approval, a particular stimulus she can provide, is a discriminative
stimulus for other important reinforcers: cookies, permission to
play outside or to stay overnight at a friend's house, the purchase
of a bicycle, etc. Still later, he may learn that possession of a
car is an important discriminative stimulus for others' behaviors
reinforcing to him—it is a stimulus which brings him the respect
and approval of his teenage peers, the ability to move fast and
far for entertainment, and an entry to lover's lane. In short, we
can say a great deal about child development simply by attending to the discriminations the child makes as he grows, since
these discriminative stimuli will control, and in part explain, his
behavior.

Typically, we will find that when a child learns that a certain
discriminative stimulus marks reinforcement occasions, he will
behave under the control of that discriminative stimulus and
also of other stimuli which are similar to it. For example, a young
toddler may be powerfully reinforced by candy. Suppose that
Father often brings home a little bag of candy, and, on arriving,
calls out "Candy!" The toddler will soon learn to approach Father
very quickly when he hears him call "Candy," since this is a
distinctive social stimulus which sets an occasion when the
behavior of approaching Father will be positively reinforced.
Prior to this experience, the spoken word "Candy" was undoubtedly a neutral stimulus for this toddler, controlling none of his

behaviors in a functional way. Now, as a consequence of its discriminative status for positive reinforcement following an approach response, we find it a powerful stimulus in controlling some of the child's behavior. In addition, we will probably find that other sounds which resemble this "Candy" will also set the occasion for a quick approach to Father. An example might be provided by Father calling upstairs to Mother, "Can you bring my jacket down?". The loud "Can. . ." may be sufficiently like the "Candy!" which has been the discriminative stimulus to set the occasion for a delighted charge toward Father by the toddler. For a time, many loud words with an initial K sound may serve as generalized discriminative stimuli.

In brief, whenever some particular stimulus, through association with reinforcement, takes on discriminative stimulus properties, then other stimuli (even though not associated directly with the reinforcement) will also take on discriminative stimulus properties, to the extent that they are similar to the original discriminative stimulus. This phenomenon is called *operant stimulus generalization.*

Generalization may be thought of as the failure to discriminate. That is, one discriminative stimulus has marked reinforcement occasions; other stimuli have not. However, because some of these other stimuli are like this first discriminative stimulus in some respect, they are responded to by the child as if they too signal an occasion for the same reinforcement. Thus, the child is not discriminating as accurately as he might. We would expect that with repeated experiences in which the original discriminative stimulus is associated with reinforcement, and other merely similar stimuli are experienced but are not followed by reinforcement, discrimination would improve. That is, the similar but unreinforced stimuli would lose their power to control behavior, while the original and reinforced discriminative stimulus would keep its power. Typically, this is true.

This process could be described systematically in terms of the strengthening of the response through reinforcement and the weakening of the response through extinction (nonreinforcement—p. 38). Reinforcing a response in the presence of particular stimuli, as we have just said, makes it more likely to occur in a wide range of similar stimulus situations. However, repeated emission of the response in these other situations without reinforcing consequences leads to the extinction of the response—in these other stimulus situations. Meanwhile, repeated emission of the response in the original stimulus situation increases and maintains the strength of the response—in the original stimulus situation. Hence it is obvious that strengthening and weakening operations can affect a response simultaneously in specific stimulus situations. Such operations, therefore, should not be thought of as necessarily affecting the strength of the response in general. In summary, then to give an operant a high probability of occurrence in a specific (discriminative) stimulus situation and a low probability of occurrence in all other stimulus situations, it is necessary to strengthen it in the discriminative stimulus situation and to extinguish it in all other situations.

To the extent that this can be done, the response will become finely discriminated to the specific discriminative stimulus desired. This is one of the meanings of "skill." Another meaning of "skill" involves choosing one response to reinforce, while extinguishing all other responses, even though they are similar to the desired response. *Just as stimuli generalize, so do responses.* Strengthening one response directly results in an indirect strengthening of other responses, insofar as they are like the original response. This is called *response generalization.* However, any response which grows in strength because it is like a reinforced response can be separately extinguished, leaving a precise form of response in the child. This is called *response differentiation.*

Learning to hit a baseball involves both stimulus discrimination and response differentiation. When a boy swings at a ball pitched within his reach, the chain of responses involved is reinforced and strengthened by occasional hits. When he swings at a ball thrown outside of his range, the motor sequence constituting the act is extinguished by a high frequency of misses. (More often it is punished by teammates and spectators.) Thus the boy's batting becomes more accurate; that is, he swings more frequently at pitches which are likely to be hit. Further refinement usually follows. A particular pitch within hitting range (like one over the plate and waist-high) may come to evoke a particular swing which "connects with" the ball. This precise swing is reinforced and strengthened, while others which are somewhat like it (but different in so far as they do not hit the ball) are extinguished or punished. Thus, batting becomes ever more precise, in that a given pitch (discriminative stimulus) is soon responded to with a particular swing (differentiated response) which is most likely to hit the ball.

We said that a large part of child development involves learning the discriminative stimuli which mark important reinforcement occasions. Another way of saying the same thing, but approaching it from the opposite direction, is to point out that a large part of child development is learning how far to generalize.

Keller and Schoenfeld[5] make two intriguing comments about the adaptive function of generalization and discrimination: "In the ever changing environment, the generalization of stimuli gives stability and consistency to our behavior . . . in contrast with generalization, the process of discrimination gives our behavior its specificity, variety, and flexibility."

ACQUIRED REINFORCEMENT

Consider again the example of the boy who learned that Father's frown was a discriminative stimulus marking a time when a request for an increase in allowance either would not be reinforced or would be negatively reinforced. By recognizing Father's frown as a discriminative stimulus for probable nonreinforcement, we understood why the youngster did not then ask for money; we predicted that he would wait for the occurrence of different discriminative stimuli (e.g., Father smiling, his feet up, reading the sports page, and smoking his pipe) which would signal a different and more favorable reinforcement

5 Fred S. Keller and William N. Schoenfeld. *Principles of psychology.* New York: Appleton-Century-Crofts, Inc., 1950, pp. 116-117.

possibility. Another prediction is reasonable: if the child could discover a better way than simply waiting for Father's frown to be replaced with a smile, he would certainly follow such a course, and then, producing the "right" discriminative stimulus from Father, he would proceed with his request. In systematic terms, if any response removed the discriminative stimulus for extinction or negative reinforcement (the frown), it would therefore be strengthened; if any response resulted in a discriminative stimulus for positive reinforcement (like a smile), that response too would be strengthened. Just this "fishing" for desirable discriminative stimuli may be observed often. But these contingencies themselves are exactly the tests establishing stimuli as reinforcers: if a response which produces a stimulus is strengthened thereby, then that stimulus is a positive reinforcer; if a response which removes or avoids a stimulus is strengthened thereby, then that stimulus is a negative reinforcer. Can a stimulus have both discriminative and reinforcing properties? According to the definitions given, it must be possible.

Our definitions, then, coupled with readily observable facts of behavior, lead to this formulation: when a stimulus acquires a discriminative function, it acquires a reinforcing function as well. In particular, discriminative stimuli for positive reinforcement or for the removal of negative reinforcement will serve as positive reinforcers. Discriminative stimuli for the presentation of negative reinforcement, for the removal of positive reinforcement, or for extinction[6] will serve as negative reinforcers. Reinforcers, positive or negative, which have achieved their reinforcing power through prior service as discriminative stimuli are called *acquired reinforcers* to denote that a learning process was involved in producing that power. (Acquired reinforcers are often called secondary, learned, or conditioned reinforcers. All are used synonymously here.) The equation of discriminative stimulus with acquired reinforcer means that the same stimulus will serve in two functions. A presentation of a discriminative stimulus (1)

---

[6] There is a relatively small body of research indicating that discriminative stimuli for extinction serve as negative reinforcers. Therefore, this part of the statement should be considered as tentative.

reinforces any preceding operants, and (2) sets the occasion for the occurrence or non-occurrence of the particular operants whose reinforcing consequences it signalled in the past.

Previously we said that much of child development could be understood by investigating the ways in which the child learns the discriminative stimuli marking situations providing reinforcements. Now it should be clear that an important segment of child development consists of the child's learning what responses produce certain discriminative stimuli and remove or avoid other discriminative stimuli. Indeed, many of the reinforcers which explain a good deal of our social behavior have the flavor of acquired reinforcers, such as approval and disapproval, social status, prestige, attention, and affection. Much of child psychology consists of analyzing the child's personal history to show where and how such stimuli first served as discriminative stimuli for other, earlier reinforcers, such as milk. An analysis along these lines goes a long way towards describing and explaining what is commonly called the child's "personality."

Recall that the soundest way to determine whether a stimulus is a reinforcer is to test its effect on some operant response which precedes it or escapes it. Now we see that in many cases we can make a fair prediction about the reinforcing qualities of a stimulus. In general, whenever a stimulus has been discriminative for reinforcement, that stimulus very likely (but not certainly) will acquire reinforcing value itself. It is still necessary to test its reinforcing value to be certain. But if investigation of the role a stimulus plays in the environment shows that it has been discriminative for reinforcement, then that stimulus is a probable candidate for testing as an acquired reinforcer.

It follows from this discussion that to make a neutral stimulus into a reinforcing stimulus, some already effective reinforcer must be available first. Then not all of the reinforcers that are effective for an individual can be acquired ones; some must have been effective from the beginning of psychological development. The term *primary reinforcer* has often been used to denote these original reinforcing stimuli. However, since relatively little is known about why primary reinforcers work, it is difficult to give a better definition of them than that they seem to be reinforcing without any history of acquisition of their reinforcing power. For our purposes, it will be enough to discover what stimuli are effective reinforcers for the infant at any moment in his development, and to trace further development from that basis. Whether these reinforcers are primary or acquired need not be critical to the learning that will be produced through their future role in the child's environment. Some of the important reinforcers which are probably primary and thus basic to future development include milk (food and water in general), temperature, rest, oxygen, and pressure (as from hard, heavy, and sharp objects).

A comparison of the acquired reinforcing value of a stimulus for operant behavior and the acquired eliciting value of a stimulus for respondent behavior may be helpful at this point. Procedurally, the two are similar: to endow a stimulus with acquired eliciting value, we present a neutral stimulus just before a stimulus which already has eliciting value for some respondent (i.e., we perform respondent conditioning). To give a stimulus acquired reinforcing value, we present a neutral stimulus on occasions when a stimulus which already has reinforcing value for an operant response is either presented or removed. This similarity in correlating two stimulus events (one neutral; one powerful in some way) is sometimes referred to in psychology as S-S (stimulus to stimulus) conditioning. However, certain critical differences between the respondent and operant cases must be kept in mind. A stimulus which has acquired eliciting properties for some respondent behavior will not control other respondents, nor will it necessarily influence any operants it might follow. A stimulus which has acquired reinforcing value will be effective in influencing *any* other operants which precede it or which remove it from the individual's environment. These differences may be obscured, however, when we deal with a stimulus which has, simultaneously, *both* eliciting value for some respondent *and* reinforcing value for any operant. Electric shock is a classic example. Electric shock elicits certain respondent behaviors (muscle contraction in the shocked part of the body, perhaps a sudden gasp, and a vocalization like "ouch!"); it also acts as a negative reinforcer, weakening operants which result in electric shock, strengthening operants which avoid or escape it. A neutral stimulus presented immediately before the onset of electric shock may simultaneously acquire eliciting and reinforcing powers. It can have eliciting power over the same respondents that the shock itself elicits, and reinforcing power over any operants which remove it or escape it. Another example from the environment of the human infant is afforded by a mother nursing her baby. The sight of Mother and her vocalizations would initially be considered neutral social stimuli. But she is present on occasions when respondents are elicited and when reinforcing stimuli are presented. For example, Mother presents the eliciting stimulus of her nipple (or a bottle's nipple) for respondent sucking; she also provides milk, an example of a positive reinforcer. Consequently, as a social stimulus, Mother should simultaneously acquire eliciting value for sucking, and reinforcing value for any operants the baby may emit. And, indeed, it is a standard observation that hungry infants do show anticipatory sucking when picked up by Mother (testifying to her acquired eliciting power), and also come to "love" Mother (testifying to her acquired reinforcing power).

Previously, it was pointed out that when a stimulus becomes discriminative for reinforcement, generalization may be expected: other stimuli, to the extent that they are similar to the stimulus discriminative for reinforcement, also take on discriminative properties. Since a discriminative stimulus is functionally equivalent to an acquired reinforcer, then just as the discriminative aspects of a stimulus will generalize, so will its reinforcing characteristic. For instance, a mother's attention may be a complex social stimulus which is discriminative for food and other reinforcement for her infant. Consequently, her attention will serve as an acquired social reinforcer. But it will generalize, too, in such a way that the attention of many other people also will reinforce operant behavior almost as well for that child. It is apparent that a child can be controlled not only by reinforcing stimuli provided by parents, but by the reinforcers supplied by other persons as well (like schoolteachers). Generalization explains much of this phenomenon.

PATTERNS IN THE REINFORCEMENT OF OPERANT BEHAVIOR: SCHEDULES OF REINFORCEMENT

An analysis of the patterns of contingencies between operants and their reinforcers will help us to understand better some of the specific characteristics of individual behavior. We are still dealing with the basic reinforcement procedures. However, we shall give our attention to some variations in these procedures, known as *schedules of reinforcement*.

The question involved here is this: Is a response reinforced *every time* it occurs? There can be a variety of answers to this question, each one defining a different schedule of reinforcement. The answer may be that the response *is* reinforced every time it occurs. This is known as a schedule of *continuous reinforcement*. It has two characteristics of interest. (1) This schedule produces a regular pattern of responding when the response produces positive reinforcement or removes negative reinforcement. (2) If a response is extinguished after continuous reinforcement, it returns to its operant level rather quickly, relatively speaking, but there are irregular recurrences of the response in considerable strength during this extinction process.

The continuous schedule of reinforcement is the basic schedule for the first systematic strengthening of a response in an individual's reinforcement history. The initial phase of teaching is usually done by continuous reinforcement for efficiency. It is not typical of the ways in which people reinforce other people, except when one person is deliberately trying to teach a new response to someone else, especially a child. Otherwise we are not liable to offer reinforcement for every response. Instead, because we ourselves are involved in other activities at the time, we tend to give reinforcers in a rather haphazard way for what we consider correct or desirable responses. Studies have been made of the effects of such *intermittent reinforcement* of operant behavior, and significant findings have come to light. Some of these will be seen to have special relevance for us in our attempt to understand the development of the child through analysis of his reinforcement history.

One way in which a response may be intermittently reinforced is by making reinforcement contingent upon the *amount of response output*. That is, the response is reinforced every Nth time it occurs. A manufacturer might pay his employee 10¢ for every twentieth unit he produces (this is known as "piecework"); a "one-armed bandit" might pay off with a jack-pot (of perhaps $10) for approximately every 100 quarters put in it. Both of these practices reinforce the responder on the basis of how many responses he has made, and are called *ratio schedules*. (That is, there will be a ratio of N responses to one reinforcer.) The effect of a ratio schedule, as might be guessed from these examples, is to generate a great deal of rapid responding for a rather small amount of reinforcement. The manufacturer who pays his employee 10¢ for every twentieth unit produced is interested in getting many responses (work) from the employee in a short period of time. His use of a ratio schedule is a shrewd one, because this is exactly the effect of ratio schedules. In particular, the higher the ratio, the faster the rate of response it produces (one reinforcement per twenty responses is a "higher" ratio than one reinforcement per ten responses).

The two examples given above differ in one important respect. Giving 10¢ for every 20 pieces of work achieved is a perfectly predictable reinforcement situation, in that the reinforcement comes at fixed points. This is an example of a *fixed ratio schedule*. On the other hand, when "a one-armed bandit" gives back money reinforcement, it does not do it on a predictable response. Instead, it reinforces the player for response output, but in a random pattern around an average ratio. The machine might be set to reinforce the player, on the average, for every 100 quarters put into it. In practice, it might reinforce (pay off) for the 97th quarter, then the 153rd, then the 178th, then the 296th, then the 472nd, then the 541st, then the 704th, etc. The average ratio of such a series might be one reinforcement per 100 responses, but the number of unreinforced responses between reinforcements is variable. It is therefore called a *variable ratio schedule.* Its effect is still to generate a high rate of responding, as do fixed ratio schedules. But if reinforcement finally stops altogether (extinction), then response after variable ratio reinforcement proves more durable than response after fixed ratio reinforcement, and much more durable than response after continuous reinforcement. These facts are particularly relevant to child development, since there are many situations in which the child will be reinforced on a ratio basis. We will be better able to understand the child's behavior patterns in those situations if we keep in mind the rate of response and its durability after reinforcement stops. A child may be on a fixed ratio schedule in school. He may be assigned 50 arithmetic problems, and told that when he is done, he can do something else (presumably something reinforcing). We would expect a fast rate of response. A child at home may be told that he must finish his homework assignment before he can go out. Again, we would expect a fast rate, because this is a fixed ratio—so many pages read to one reinforcement. (Note that "pages read" and "pages comprehended" are two different behaviors.) A young child may discover that when Mother is watching her favorite TV program, he must ask her many times for something he wants before he can crack through Mother's shell of preoccupation. This is variable ratio. If this is a frequent occurrence, we may expect that repetitive requests at a rapid rate will become a strong response characteristic of the child, and that if he is put on a different reinforcement schedule, or is no longer reinforced, the response will be slow to extinguish.

We turn now to a different way in which responses may be intermittently reinforced. Here, the answer to the question of scheduling (Is a response reinforced every time it occurs?) is that the response will be reinforced the first time it occurs after N minutes since the last time it was reinforced. In other words, we may reinforce responses on the basis of *time passing* rather than of response output. A schedule constructed on this basis is called an *interval schedule,* to denote its reliance upon a period of time intervening between any two reinforcements. An employer might pay his employees every Friday afternoon. A professor might reinforce studying in his students with a quiz every Monday. A mother might decide that her toddler can have the cookie requested, because it has been "long enough" since the last one. In all of these examples, it is not response output which determines the next reinforcement occasion, but simply the passage of time, and time cannot be hurried by responding. However, the reinforcement is not given "free"; it is given as a consequence of a response—the first response occurring after a given time has passed since the last reinforcement.

An interval schedule in which the time between reinforced responses is not constant is essential in understanding a child's behavior. The example above, in which Mother gives her child a cookie upon request simply because it has been "long enough" since the last cookie, shows just such a *variable interval* schedule. An interesting characteristic of variable interval schedules is that they produce extremely durable responses, ones which will continue to be emitted at a slow, even rate long after reinforcement has ceased. This suggests that behaviors strengthened through reinforcement on variable interval schedules may be depended upon to survive for long periods without reinforcement, or to maintain themselves when reinforcement is exceedingly irregular and infrequent. A child will show many behaviors which are emitted at slow rates, perhaps only a few times a day, which seem only rarely to be reinforced in any way the observer can detect, and yet which retain their strength. Very often, the explanation of such behaviors may lie precisely in the variable interval schedule on which they are now, or have been in the past, reinforced.

The nagging behavior of a child (begging, whining speech, sleeve tugging, and the like) is a response which sometimes is reinforced on a variable ratio schedule (i.e., when the child has nagged enough times, the parent gives in), but which often is reinforced on a variable interval basis: when the parent thinks it has been "long enough" since the last reinforcement, he gives in, or when the child does it in public, or when the parent is tired. The interval often may be a long one, on the average, particularly when the parent thinks he is going to discourage nagging by not giving in. In principle, this is sound—if nagging is never reinforced, it will extinguish. But the typical parent may not quite manage *never* to reinforce nagging; instead, on rare occasions, in moments of weakness, he may succumb. The effect of these occasional reinforcements is to generate a history of variable interval reinforcement of the nagging response, which contribues greatly to its strength and durability. Consequently, even if the parent should manage never again to reinforce nagging in the future, it will be a long time and many responses until it finally extinguishes. Even *one* reinforcement during this extinction process may re-establish the response in considerable strength.

This example shows how a behavior may persist for a long period, even with a minimum of reinforcement, because of its past schedule of reinforcement. Very often, in talking about the personality of a child, traits are pointed to which are durable and persistent in that child's behavior, but which have no obvious and plentiful source of reinforcement in the child's current environment. Nagging, temper tantrums, and whining are typical examples. The explanation of many personality characteristics of this sort may lie in a past history of reinforcement on a variable interval basis.

Both ratio and interval schedules support a great deal of behavior with a small amount of reinforcement. Ratio schedules may generate many hundreds of responses for each reinforcement, and at a rapid rate; interval schedules may generate moderate but stable rates of response over many hours between reinforcements. But a point worth emphasizing is that these extremely "stretched out" schedules cannot be imposed successfully at the beginning of learning. They must be developed gradually from reinforcement schedules in which responses, at least at first, are reinforced nearly every time they occur—continuous reinforcement. Once a response has been strengthened by continuous or nearly continuous reinforcement, the schedule then may shift through a series of increasing ratios or increasing intervals, to the point where an extremely powerful, stable, or durable response exists, maintained by a minimal amount of reinforcement. One of the most powerful tools available for analyzing the child's psychological development may be this concept of developing strong, stable responses upon gradually shifting, "thinning-out" schedules of reinforcement.

Still another important interval schedule is one with *aversive* characteristics. In this learning situation, the response avoids the presentation of a negative reinforcer. For example, a child may notice an ominous frown on the face of his mother, and quickly volunteer to wash the dishes. Perhaps this will erase the frown, which to the child is a discriminative stimulus for impending negative reinforcement like a bawling out or a restriction of privileges. But the effect of this removal may be temporary. In time, it may appear that another "helpful" response is necessary to delay another imminent blow-up of the parent. Studies have been made of aversive schedules which produce a negative reinforcer at fixed time intervals (e.g., every 30 seconds), unless a certain response is made. When the effect of the response is to put off the impending negative reinforcement for another period of time (say another 30 seconds), then this contingency between a response and the delay of the next negative reinforcement is sufficient gradually to build up the strength of the response. In fact, the response often increases in strength (in experimental situations) to the point where it successfully avoids virtually all of the scheduled negative reinforcements. In this case, we see a response made at a steady rate, apparently very durable, but we do not see any reinforcement supporting the response. The reason for this apparent independence of the response from reinforcement is, of course, that the response is maintained because it avoids negative reinforcement. The response may be closely tied to a particular discriminative stimulus like a frown or may only be controlled by the less obvious stimulus provided by the passage of time. For example, a parent who is frequently angry (but in an unpredictable way) may be placated often by his children during the day, just because it has been "a while" since his last outburst, a stimulus which is discriminative for the next one coming up soon. The placating response may then be viewed as one which is maintained because it avoids negative reinforcement, that is, it is reinforced on an aversive schedule.

The aversive schedule is often an essential characteristic of some social situations, because it sets up extremely strong and durable responses which persist without obvious reinforcement—they are successful responses exactly because they keep the reinforcement from becoming obvious. An example is saying "You're welcome." Saying it would not get us much, but omitting it would. Thus this schedule, like the other schedules discussed, promises to be useful in analyzing many childhood interactions.

We have provided only a small sample of the ways in which scheduling may be involved in the control of behavior. Knowing what schedule has been operating is very useful in understanding what happens in a large number of the child's reinforcement situations. However, it should be remembered that in the child's everyday reinforcement experiences, these schedules are intermixed and combined in complex ways.

THE EFFECTS OF DEPRIVATION AND SATIATION (SETTING EVENTS) ON REINFORCERS

In the Introduction we stated that the environment consists of *specific stimuli* and of *setting events*. Our discussion thus far has centered about stimuli and their functions, especially those with reinforcing and discriminative properties. Now we are ready to fit into this picture two kinds of setting conditions which have received considerable research attention: deprivation and satiation of reinforcers.

Let us start with an example. Food is probably a primary reinforcer, that is, one not acquired through operant discriminative learning or through respondent conditioning. Yet there are obvious times when food will not reinforce—just after a large meal, or during stomach upsets, for example. There are other reinforcers (e.g., water, air), the effectiveness of which varies as a function of many things, one of them again being how much of the reinforcer the organism has had recently.

We can now state a formal principle: the reinforcing power of many (not all) reinforcers depends upon their supply or availability to the organism *over a period of time*. When an organism has not had such a reinforcer for a long period, it may be said to be in a state of deprivation. On the other hand, when the organism very recently has consumed a large amount of a reinforcer, it may be said to be *satiated*. The mark of complete satiation is the failure of the reinforcer to strengthen behavior, that is, to strengthen any operant responses. The effect of deprivation, on the other hand, is to increase the effectiveness of a reinforcer to control operant behavior.

Probably, the effectiveness of many reinforcers, the unlearned or primary as well as the learned or aquired kind, is subject to the effects of deprivation or satiation. We can be sure that deprivation and satiation operations will have an effect only by making the proper tests upon each reinforcing stimulus we are interested in studying. Similarly, we shall expect that different reinforcers will show different sensitivity to deprivation-satiation operations for different children. If a child is accustomed to getting a great deal of supporting approval and attention from its parents, even an hour of being ignored by them may noticeably increase the reinforcing effectiveness of their approval and attention. For another child, who gets much less attention from his parents, several hours of being ignored might be required to produce the same increased effectiveness. Similarly, it might require dozens of closely spaced instances of attention and approval to satiate the first child, and relatively few to satiate the second.

THE SIMULTANEOUS APPLICATION OF OPPOSING STIMULUS FUNCTIONS: CONFLICT

At this point, we have covered a fair amount of detail in describing the dynamics of operant behavior. It is apparent, now, that to understand the occurrence or nonoccurrence of an operant we need to know at least the following:

1. The stimulus function of the consequences of this response: the production or removal of positive or negative reinforcers, or of neutral stimuli (p. 33).

2. The promptness with which this stimulus function is applied, now and in the past (p. 43).

3. The extent to which particular discriminative stimuli have accompanied this response and its stimulus consequences (p. 48).

4. The history of the stimulus function involved: whether it is a learned or unlearned reinforcer; and, if learned, the details of the learning process (p. 53).

5. The schedule according to which the operant produces or avoids this or a similar stimulus consequence (p. 58).

6. The number of times the response has had a similar stimulus consequence (that is, one with a similar stimulus function) in the past (p. 45).

7. The deprivation or satiation status of the child for this stimulus, if relevant (p. 64).

Despite the relative wealth of detail which is applicable in an analysis, the discussion so far has been in terms of the simplest possible case, in which a clearly discriminated operant produces a stimulus consequence with a single reinforcing function. Consider now the possibilities of operants not so clearly discriminated, or producing two (or more) stimulus consequences, with opposing, contradictory reinforcing functions.

1. An operant may simultaneously produce a positive reinforcer *and* a negative reinforcer. The effect of the former is to strengthen the operant, and of the latter, to weaken it.

2. An operant may produce one positive reinforcer and simultaneously lose or avoid other positive reinforcers. Again, one stimulus function strengthens, the other weakens the response.

3. An operant may produce one negative reinforcer and simultaneously avoid another negative reinforcer. Again, the effects of these stimulus consequences upon the response are opposed.

4. An operant may lose a positive reinforcer and simultaneously avoid or escape a negative reinforcer. Again, the effects of these stimulus functions are also contradictory.

5. The above possibilities are ways in which a single response may have contradictory consequences. But we might as realistically consider situations in which *two or more* operants are possible, each with contradictory stimulus consequences. (We will consider an example in detail presently.)

6. A response may have contradictory stimulus consequences, but at different times. For example, a response may be positively reinforced immediately but negatively reinforced later. "Fly now, pay later" is one such application. "Drink now, get sick later" is another. The child who watches TV in the evening when he should be studying for a spelling test scheduled for the next morning, is still another.

7. There may be a conflict between the functions of discriminative stimuli present at the time, if these stimuli set the occasion for later contradictory reinforcements. The child who watches TV when he should be studying is receiving positive reinforcement (the TV program) at the moment, but he is not failing his test at the same time—that is a reinforcement event which is to take place the next day. However, he is in the presence of a discriminative stimulus setting the occasion for negative reinforcement (test failure) the next day: time is passing without study, a stimulus situation which the reader well knows to be discriminative for poor grades at the end of the term. Thus a child may be in conflict simply by being in the presence of discriminative stimuli which promise later reinforcements of contradictory kinds.[7]

8. There may be conflict because the discriminative stimuli present at the moment are unclear or confused, in terms of his past history of reinforcement in their presence. When someone calls you an idiot, but smiles as he says it, are you being positively or negatively reinforced? If the stimuli are too novel to you in that combination, you may be in conflict.

[7] Remember that discriminative stimuli function as acquired reinforcers (p. 54). Thus a conflict between opposing discriminative stimuli is, in this sense, a conflict between reinforcers present *at the moment*.

What will happen when a response has consequences which simultaneously act to weaken and strengthen it, or when contradictory or ambiguous discriminative stimuli are presented? The answer is implicit in the summary list of principles which introduced this section. It is necessary to discover the strength of each stimulus function, its power in affecting the operant, and then to compare the strength of the two opposing functions. How is the strength of a stimulus function assessed or measured? Largely by the details which comprise points 2 through 7 of that list.

This is the common sense answer. When a person is caught between the devil and the deep blue sea, he is liable to ask just these pertinent questions before finally choosing. How strong is the devil? How hot is his fire? What is my present temperature? How cold is the deep blue sea? How good am I at swimming?

The child's everyday life contains many situations in which opposing stimulus functions are unavoidable. For example, consider the boy who has been told that he will get $3 for cutting the grass, which must be cut today, and then discovers that his gang is having an important baseball game today with a rival bunch. In this illustration there are at least two operants, each of which has opposing stimulus consequences. The boy may cut the grass. This response produces $3, a definite positive reinforcer, but loses him participation in the ball game, a loss of both fun and approval from his peers, which are positive social reinforcers. The $3 should promote grass-cutting, the loss of fun and approval from peers should weaken it. On the other hand, the boy may go to the game. In this case, he has a good deal of fun and receives peer approval, but does not obtain the $3. When he gets home, he probably will encounter his parents' angry disapproval, and perhaps lose other reinforcers such as his allowance or some other privileges. The fun and peer approval should promote ball playing, but the loss of the money, the parental disapproval, and the potential loss of other reinforcers should weaken ball playing.

To find out what the boy will do, we need a great deal of information about him and his situation. In fact, we need exactly the kind of information outlined in the list at the beginning of this section (p. 65). For example: one basic reinforcer involved is the $3. What is his deprivation condition for dollars? What does the boy mean to buy with it? What is his deprivation state for that? Peer approval is another basic reinforcer involved here. What is the boy's deprivation state for this stimulus? What is his usual schedule of peer reinforcement? What in his history establishes peer approval as a reinforcer? How powerful is the alternative parental approval which can compete with peer approval? What is its schedule? Its deprivation state? Its history of acquisition?

The answers to these and similar questions obviously contribute to a sort of bookkeeping of debits and credits for the stimulus functions involved. The final answer will follow from an adding up of the plus and minus factors for each response, to see which will control the operant. An important problem in psychology, clearly enough, is to devise methods of measuring these factors which will assign definite numbers to them.

However, the point most worthy of emphasis here is that conflict is not a special topic involving new principles. The principles involved in conflict are the same as those in simpler situations involving operants; but they are applied in more complex combinations. The accounting may be difficult, but it is not, in principle, impossible, and the values involved may be lawfully determined.

Two points might seem to make conflict a special situation. The first is the possibility, at least in theory, of finding a conflict situation in which the opposing stimulus functions exactly balance each other; so that the stimulus consequence tending to strengthen the response is exactly as powerful as the stimulus consequence tending to weaken it. In this case, we may observe the child vacillating between the alternatives, choosing neither for more than a short period of time. The boy in our previous example might, if the stimuli were exactly balanced, start cutting the grass, then after a few minutes give it up, get his baseball glove, and start for the game; but halfway there he might stop, mutter to himself, and head back home to cut some more grass.

And then, halfway through the lawn, he might again get his glove and go to the game, and actually play a few innings. (After all, with the grass half cut, the parental disapproval he is risking well may be less severe than if none of the grass were cut.) After playing a few innings, especially if his team is well ahead, the possibility of $3 might prove reinforcing enough to start him home again to finish the grass. (And after all, he has had some fun, and his peers probably will not disapprove of him for leaving when the game seems won anyway.) Thus, in special cases, conflict can produce a back-and-forth behavior which, at first glance, may seem like a special kind of response, unlike anything discussed so far. However, it is readily explained by the same principles that explain operant behaviors in general. Each activity alters the deprivation condition for its reinforcer, and so destroys the balance between them.

The second point about conflict which might make it seem a special problem is this: when a child is placed in a situation where a response will have stimulus consequences with opposing functions, he may show a certain amount of "emotional" behavior. That is, we may say that he seems "frustrated," or "torn" by the conflict, or, more loosely, "all hung up." Much of this follows from the fact that very often in conflict situations the child must accept negative reinforcement in order to get more powerful positive reinforcement, or he must lose positive reinforcement in order to escape or avoid more powerful negative reinforcement. The presentation of negative reinforcers, or the loss of positive reinforcers, has a close connection with what is usually called "emotional" behavior; but emotional behavior is a topic of its own. We consider it next. The point here is that the conflict behavior is itself explainable, and is not a new subject matter.

6

Operant–Respondent Relations and Emotional Behavior

ANALYSIS OF PSYCHOLOGICAL INTERACTIONS INVOLVING BOTH OPERANTS AND RESPONDENTS

Thus far, we have dealt with operants and respondents separately, emphasizing the difference in the laws describing the dynamics of each. Without abridging the significance of these differences, we now shift to a more complex level. Typically, operant and respondent behaviors occur together in a child's everyday behavior, and they may interact in intricate ways. To understand these patterns requires observing the effects of the operant behaviors on the respondents, and at the same time the effects of the respondents on the operants.

Consider again the behavior involved in obtaining food. A child, in a mild state of deprivation, may approach Mother and ask for a cookie. The cookie is reinforcing, and the operant response ("Gimme a cookie") has been reinforced by cookies in past stimulus situations involving Mother as a discriminative stimulus; this explains the child's behavior. So far the analysis has used only operant principles. Note, however, that as the child is given the cookie, he is liable to salivate. This interaction would be a conditioned respondent. The taste of the cookie (like the taste of almost any food) serves as an eliciting stimulus for the respondent of salivation. The *sight* of cookies once had no eliciting power for salivation, but because it has almost invariably been associated with the taste of cookies in the child's history, it has acquired eliciting power. The respondent of salivation has become conditioned to the sight of a cookie. So here is one respondent intertwined with the ongoing operant behavior of asking, reaching, and chewing.

Furthermore, this respondent salivation inevitably provides stimulation to the child: he feels the increased saliva in his mouth. This stimulus must have served as a cue on past occasions for putting the cookie in the mouth and being reinforced. Hence, the respondent provides the child with an added discriminative stimulus for continuing the series of operant responses. The sight of the cookie and the feel of it in his hand are discriminative stimuli, and so is increased salivation, for the response of putting the cookie in the mouth.

Consider another example: swallowing, and the resulting wave of peristaltic contractions of the child's esophagus which passes the chewed cookies down to the stomach. The chain of operant behaviors starting with the child's request for the cookie will end in a long chain of respondents, starting with peristalsis and continuing with the internal responses making up the digestive process, all of which are characterized as respondents.

Note that some psychologists usually lose interest in the child's behavior at the point when the child puts the cookie in his mouth. The child has not stopped behaving; the psychologist has. In effect, the psychologist may arbitrarily stop studying this complex chain of operants and respondents at some point which he recognizes as one of the rough boundaries of his field, leaving the rest of the chain to be studied by physiologists and other biologists. However, if the cookie were to cause a stomach ache, the psychologist would again be interested. (Recall the discussion of the role of organismic variables on p. 10)

And finally, we may expect that a young child, given a cookie, may very well smile and laugh; he will seem "pleased." These behaviors have a large respondent component which is a notable characteristic of this reinforcement situation. We may generalize from this example that most operant chains will be intermixed with respondent chains. Indeed, if we pursue this line of analysis in the interests of a more complete description of the child's everyday behavior, we come to an imprecise but thoroughly important principle about respondents and reinforcing stimuli, which we develop in the next section.

EMOTIONAL BEHAVIOR

The behavior popularly called emotional can be analyzed as respondent in nature. Hence, any such emotional response is not affected by reinforcing stimuli which follow it, but instead is controlled by eliciting stimuli preceding it. However, these eliciting stimuli often prove to be reinforcing stimuli (for other operant behaviors). Thus, the process of reinforcing a child, by any of the procedures previously discussed (see Table I, page 37), may elicit respondent behavior from him, too. Consider these examples:

A child being scolded may blush. Blushing is a respondent behavior elicited by the presentation of a negative reinforcer (disapproval) in this case. A layman is liable to say the child is "ashamed."

A child wakes up Christmas morning, runs to the tree, and discovers the bicycle he has wanted for more than a year. He may break into goose pimples, flush, breathe faster; in short, a layman might say he is "thrilled." The respondents involved here are elicited by the sudden presentation of a positive reinforcer which is very powerful due to a prolonged period of deprivation.

Take a cookie away from a baby. He is liable to burst into loud cries and tears almost immediately. These are respondent behaviors elicited by the sudden removal of a positive reinforcer. In everyday language we would say the baby is "angry."

Mother may tell her nine-year-old daughter that she need not wash the dishes tonight. Perhaps the girl will smile, giggle, and whoop as she dashes off. We might say that she is "relieved." From a systematic point of view, we refer to respondents elicited by the unexpected removal of a negative reinforcer.

Finally, consider the toddler whose mother has locked the recreation room door because there is broken glass on the floor

The child stands outside the door, reaches for the knob, turns it, and pushes; but the door does not move. The child may then tug violently at the door, cry, and shout. These behaviors involve several respondents which are elicited largely because an operant previously reinforced every time it occurred, for many times in the child's history with door knobs, is now being extinguished for the first time. That is, for once the child is turning and pushing on the knob, but the door is not opening—he is not getting the usual reinforcing stimulation provided by being able to control the door and get to the toys on the other side. We might say the child is "frustrated," but we only mean that he displays certain emotional respondents as a result of a failure of reinforcement.

These examples show that any of the basic reinforcement operations and extinction procedures may also elicit respondent behaviors. We tend to label these respondents "emotional" *largely because of the nature of the reinforcement situations which give rise to them.* When a hot room leads to dilation of the blood vessels on the surface of the skin, and a person becomes flushed, we do not usually call this an emotional response; but when a scolding leads to the same dilation of the same blood vessels, we tend to say that the child is blushing with shame and hence is emotional. The respondent has not changed, but the eliciting stimulus situation has. Emotional responses, then, are respondent responses to particular kinds of eliciting stimulation: usually to stimulation made up of reinforcing stimuli, positive or negative, being presented or removed, or the beginning of extinction.

Recall now the preceding section on conflict. The final point made in that section was that conflict often seemed to involve a distinctive emotional content—being "torn" by conflict. Now it should be clear that much of the emotional behavior involved in conflict can be explained by the fact that to endure or resolve a conflict, the child typically must either receive negative rein- forcement (perhaps in order to get more positive reinforcement) or must lose positive reinforcement (perhaps to avoid more negative reinforcement). Such operations, as we have just seen, elicit respondent behaviors described as emotional.[1] Furthermore, in those conflict situations where the values of the opposing reinforcers are nearly equal, such that the child oscillates between one response and another, he often cannot do anything else until the conflict is resolved. Since there may be many other discriminative stimuli present for other behaviors with other reinforcing contingencies, and since these are not being responded to, even more emotional behavior may be elicited. Consider the girl asked out to a dance who cannot decide which of two dresses to wear. As she stands before her closest, temporarily incapable of choosing between the two garments, time is passing, a discriminative stimulus requiring many other responses from her if she is going to avoid the negative reinforcement of being later than usual. But the stimulus of time passing cannot be responded to, perhaps, until she settles upon one dress. If the dresses have equal reinforcing value to her, we would expect that the situation will stall her and elicit flurries of irritation and other respondents. Sometimes it is argued that reinforcers affect behavior the way they do *because* of the emotional response that they elicit. It is said that ultimately it is the emotion which is powerful; the reinforcer is effective only because it elicits emotional respondent behavior, which generates internal stimulation ("feelings"). William James' famous example[2] explaining why men run from bears can clarify this kind of reasoning. Usually, it is argued that a man runs from a bear because he is afraid of the bear; by running, the man escapes from the source of his fear. That is, the bear acts as a negative reinforcer *because* it makes the man afraid. James offered an alternative argument: a man runs from a bear because the bear is a negative reinforcer. In addition, the man is afraid *because* he is running from a negative reinforcer. We can diagram

[1] Recall the study of Jones described on p. 30. There an "emotional" stimulus (a rabbit which elicited crying) was more quickly extinguished as emotion-arousing by simultaneously making it discriminative for candy reinforcement. Operant-respondent combinations may resolve conflicts and reduce emotions as well as promote them.

[2] William James. *The principles of psychology.* Vol. 2. New York: Henry Holt and Co., 1890, pp. 149-150.

these two possibilities, and a third which is an acceptable alternative, in the following way:

Usual argument: *Bear* causes *fear* causes *running*
James' argument: *Bear* causes *running* causes *fear*
Alternative:
                     Bear ⎧ causes *running* (operant which escapes
                            ⎨   bear, a negative reinforcer)
                            ⎩ elicits *fear* (respondent)

Probably we cannot settle this argument one way or the other today. Perhaps emotions explain reinforcement effects; perhaps reinforcement effects explain emotions. We shall say here only that the two often go hand in hand, without assigning a cause and effect relationship. Let it be argued that men see bears and run because bears are discriminative stimuli for negative reinforcement (and therefore are acquired negative reinforcers themselves); *at the same time,* men are fearful because bears are acquired negative reinforcers, and the presentation of negative reinforcers is a conditioned stimulus situation eliciting the respondents which make up "fear" (the third alternative above). One thing is certain: we may observe reinforcing stimuli controlling operants in a child in their usual manner, yet we find no objective evidence of the operation of emotional respondents. This kind of observation is responsible for much research concentrating upon operant principles. As scientists, we must rely as much as possible upon *observable* stimulus and response events; when we can observe reinforcing stimuli controlling behaviors, and cannot observe emotional respondents intertwined, we tend to lean primarily upon operant rather than upon respondent principles for analysis and explanation.

SELF-CONTROL

Another interesting area of study growing out of an analysis of the interaction between operants and respondents bears on the concept of self-control. You will recall that just as external stimuli control behavior, so may internal or self-generated stimuli. That is, two sets of responses may be active at the same time, in such a way that the consequences of one influence the other. For example, Mother may take her toddler to a department store at Christmas time. On the way through the toy department, the child will be literally deluged with stimuli setting the occasion for thousands of possible responses (play) with hundreds of possible reinforcers (toys). She lets go of the child's hand to turn a price tag, and the child moves off toward a toy counter, and reaches for a particularly alluring gadget. But just as his hand is about to touch it, we *may* hear him repeating mother's thousand-times-repeated admonition, "DON'T TOUCH!" and as a consequence, his hand slowly retreats, leaving him standing there, gazing sadly at the toy. (These "sadness" respondents probably are elicited by his self-removal of a positive reinforcer.)

There are many ways in which self-generated behavior may control other responses of the same individual. A person may talk to himself about infuriating memories (i.e., occasions when positive reinforcers were lost or negative reinforcers produced) to elicit "angry" respondents that bolster his behavior for an argument or a fight. A child may wake in the middle of the night and say, "I don't have to ask to go to the potty," and then leave his bedroom for the bathroom. Without this self-generated permission, a child who is usually scolded for getting up after being put to bed might not get up, if his sleeping parents didn't hear him call, and so wet his bed. A child may say again and again, "If I'm good today, Daddy will take me to the playground after supper," and this self-reminder may actually keep the child out of a fair proportion of his usual daily misbehaviors. A common example among college students is the learned behavior of drinking vast quantities of coffee the night before a test in order to counteract sleepy responses. Coffee drinking allows studying. Another example, which has been the object of an elaborate experimental study,[3] is the self-control of overeating. Basically, eating is a food-reinforced behavior, and many persons may become satiated for food only after too many calories have been ingested to maintain a steady weight. The negative reinforcement of be-

[3] C. B. Ferster, J. I. Nurnberger, and E. E. Levitt. *The control of eating.* In preparation.

coming overweight is a stimulus event occurring long after the response causing it (overeating), and hence is not effective in weakening the behavior. Probably only through techniques of self-control can the overweight person reduce by making eating an occasion for other behaviors which may immediately punish overeating, or strengthen some competitive response, or otherwise reduce the reinforcing value of food. One example could be making eating the occasion for verbal behavior equating the food to calories and the calories to pounds. This adds an immediate negative reinforcer to the situation, which is produced by eating more and escaped from by not eating more. There are many other possibilities with the same effect.

One of the most interesting aspects of self-control from our point of view is the development of "conscience" in children. The ability of a child to behave as taught *in the absence of his teachers* has been a critical problem in personality development throughout the history of child psychology. It has given rise to theories emphasizing the self, a super-ego, or internal anxiety responses. All of these theories have in common the idea that the child learns to respond so as to produce other stimuli, which permit other desirable responses or prevent other undesirable responses. This is what we mean by saying that a child learns "to control himself."

Sometimes in the young toddler, we see misbehavior accompanied by a rather cheerful "No, no" from the toddler himself. However, with further development the "No, no" becomes less cheerful, precedes the misbehavior, and often prevents it. Why? An analysis of his history might show something like this operating: When he has committed this misdeed previously—let us say taking mother's stationery from her desk—she has taken it away from him and said "No, no." Let us suppose that this toddler has had little history with "No, no" as discriminative for punishment, and so its basic stimulus function for him lies in its identity as part of mother's attention, a positive social reinforcer. "No, no," then, is a sound marking occasions of positive social reinforcement, and takes on positive reinforcing value itself, as a consequence. Hence verbal behaviors which produce it (the child using his own vocal cords to say "No, no") are strengthened. However, this is a sound somewhat discriminated to the misdeed itself—the taking of stationery from mother's desk. So the infant is more likely to emit "No, no" when playing with the stationery in the desk, and it will be a cheerful enough operant. However, a child at this stage of development very likely is doing many things all day long which lead his mother to say "No, no" repeatedly as she stops him and rescues her valuables. Naturally enough, she is liable to take a more and more severe role in trying to modify his behavior into acceptable (nondestructive) forms. It is likely then that her "No, no" will quickly come to be a discriminative stimulus for repeated applications of punishment, both through the presentation of negative reinforcers and through the withdrawal of positive reinforcers. Thus, "No, no" will begin to change its stimulus function for this child: as it becomes more and more clearly discriminative for punishment, it will itself become a social negative reinforcer, rather than a social positive reinforcer. Therefore, as the child says "No, no" on future occasions when he investigates mother's stationery in her desk, he is accomplishing his own punishment, and his behavior weakens accordingly.

According to this analysis, there need not be any special principles invoked to analyze the development of "conscience"; the self-generated behaviors which prevent misbehavior and promote good behavior may be explained in terms of the same principles already discussed here. That is, an investigation of the child's history can show that he learns to say "No, no" in the same way that he learns all his other operants: through the action of reinforcement contingencies in which "No, no" figures as a verbal operant, strengthened typically by social reinforcement from parents, teachers, and others.

However, it should be recognized that the concept of self-control often tempts the theorist to invoke new principles. Self-control is defined as control of certain responses by stimuli produced by other responses of the same individual, that is, by self-generated stimuli. But what if these self-generated stimuli are not observable? In the example of the child who reaches for a toy but stops short of picking it up, what if we fail to hear him say "Don't touch" as he withdraws his hand? A common solution to this problem is to *infer* that some response-produced stimulation occurs internally which connects the response observed and the child's history of past learning relevant to the response. We do not wish to engage in this kind of inference. If observable responses of a child produce observable stimuli which functionally relate to other behaviors of the child, then we can talk about self-control by stating the functional relationships involved. If any of the critical responses or response-produced stimuli are not observable, then no application of the concept of self-control can justifiably be made.

Fortunately, a large part of the developing self-controlling behavior of young children is in fact observable, especially the kind consisting of verbal behavior. It is frequently observed that young children maintain a running conversation with themselves, part of which is recognizable to parents as exact quotations from their own commands to the children. More than one child has been observed to get up from a fall, wailing "I should be more careful!" In situations when it occurs earlier and earlier in play sequences, this comment could stimulate more careful behavior in the child.

These examples are common but by no means universal in young children. To the extent that they exist in observable forms, an objective analysis of the development of "conscience" and similar behaviors becomes possible through concepts of self-controlling behavior. However, to the extent that such behaviors are not observable, the concept cannot be applied, if a natural science approach to child development is to be maintained. This consideration may impose a limitation on a study of "conscience" in children, since many behaviors of this type may in fact be mediated by internal responses not observable to the psychologist in the present state of technology.[4] If these responses

4 Note that an internal response is not necessarily an unobservable response. As research in the area of physiological psychology proceeds, it is to be expected that present techniques for observing internal behavior and stimulation will be greatly improved, and new techniques developed. Hence,

are not observable, they may in fact be present and self-controlling; but they might not exist at all. We cannot insist that internal self-controlling responses exist simply because the child is moral in his behavior. There are many principles of behavior, stated in terms of observable past events, which could explain why certain "good" responses of the child are strong, and other "bad" responses weak. The point is to try to analyze behavior in terms of the variables available for study, rather than to insist that a single mechanism like self-control must be responsible for all such development and to infer its action in every case in which it cannot be directly observed.

We consider now a final example of how self-control may be established in a person (and, incidentally, a good example of one possible relationship between operant and respondent behavior in the same person). This example will consist of some techniques of training which would enable an individual to win the $100 bet on the pupillary response cited in the section on respondent behavior (p. 27). There it was argued that since the pupillary response is respondent in nature, it could not be controlled by the offer of any consequent reinforcing stimulation—not even by the offer of $100 as a consequence. The pupillary response could be elicited only by preceding stimulation. Let us prepare a friend to be able to win the bet through his own behavior by giving him a conditioned eliciting stimulus which he may present to himself. First, we condition the pupillary responses of our friend to a sound, by the usual procedure of respondent conditioning: we make the sound, and promptly shine a bright light in our subject's eyes. The bright light elicits the pupillary response, and the sound, associated with the bright light, will come to elicit the response by itself, if we repeat this procedure often enough. However, let us choose a particularly useful sound for our purpose: a spoken word, such as "psychology." That is, each time we shine the bright light in our friend's eyes, we first say aloud

present limitations to a study of internal "mediating" events may be temporary. In general, a natural science approach to psychological development is not restricted to stimulus and response events *outside* the organism; it is restricted to *observable* stimulus and response events in any locale.

"psychology." As a consequence of this conditioning, our friend is so modified that whenever he hears the word "psychology," his pupils constrict. Naturally, he too can say the word "psychology," and so he can control one of his own respondents (pupillary response) by one of his own operants (saying "psychology"), as a result of this learning experience. Then the first unwary psychologist our friend meets who offers $100 reinforcement of the pupillary response (as an example of its insensitivity to consequent stimulation) will lose his money, as our friend calls out "psychology" and his pupils constrict.

A second (and somewhat simpler) technique would be to inform our friend on some previous occasion that looking from a near point of fixation to a far away point will affect the pupillary response. A change in fixation, in fact, manipulates the amount of light falling upon the retina, and thereby manipulates the eliciting stimulation controlling the pupillary response. To give the subject this information is to teach him a chain of symbolic operant responses, which, put to use on a later occasion, causes him to move his eyes (another operant), and so affects the eliciting stimulation of light falling on the retina, which again will cost the psychologist $100 as it elicits the pupillary respondent.

In both techniques, we make it possible for an individual to use certain operant behaviors which will manipulate eliciting stimulation that controls respondent behavior. In effect, by strengthening the critical operants (saying "psychology" or memorizing the relationship between change of fixation and the pupillary response), we give the subject self-control. It should be emphasized, however, that when he displays such self-control, his behavior is still the product of his history of interaction with his past environment and of the present stimulus situation.

7

Summary—and a Look Forward

A summary of our discussion can be little more than the table of contents which preceded it. It must be clear to the reader that our presentation is, in fact, only a descriptive summary of modern empirical behavior theory. Let us then use the summary to emphasize the distinctive aspects of the volume.

An outline of descriptive principles, stated only in objective, observable terms, has been developed which can be applied to behavior in general—the behavior of young and old, human and animal, in isolated, social, and laboratory settings. A detailed application of these principles has been made to the developing human child, with the intention of introducing the reader to techniques of analyzing the interactions of the child and his world from a natural science point of view. Such an analysis should explain a great deal of our present knowledge about the sequences of child development—knowledge which we believe to be valid even while we often have been puzzled as to *why* it is true. Equally important, this approach should lead to the discovery of new and important knowledge. In short, we believe that this is one way to state what we know in this area at present and to ask questions about what we do not know.

What form does this analysis take, applied comprehensively to the whole problem of child development? Let us answer the question by outlining what is to follow in later volumes: these concepts, applied to child development, yield a rather thorough account of the development of the human child's motor, perceptual, linguistic, intellectual, emotional, social, and motivational repertoires. Indeed, these concepts suggest that the foregoing list of traits is an artificial or at least not a *functional* one, since all of these presumed faculties can be stated in their ontogenesis by various combinations of the same principles of operant and respondent behavior. The theory proceeds by the following chain:

1. The developing child is adequately conceptualized as a source of responses which fall into two functional classes: respondents, which are controlled primarily by preceding eliciting stimulation and which are largely insensitive to consequent stimulation; and operants, which are controlled primarily by consequent stimulation, their attachment to preceding (discriminative) stimuli being dependent upon the stimulus consequences of behavior previously made in the presence of these discriminative stimuli. Some responses may share attributes of both respondents and operants.

2. Initial understanding of the child's development next requires analysis of the child's environment, which is conceptualized as a source both of eliciting stimuli controlling his respondents and of reinforcing stimuli which can control his operants. Catalogues of both of these types of stimuli would be required as part of this analysis.

3. Subsequent analysis of the child's development proceeds by listing the ways in which respondents are attached to new eliciting stimuli and detached from old ones, through respondent conditioning and extinction. Similarly, a listing is made of the ways in which operants are strengthened or weakened through various reinforcement contingencies, and discriminated to various stimuli which reliably mark occasions on which these contingencies hold. Some respondents are called "emotional," and the conditioned eliciting stimuli for them may be provided by people, and hence are "social." Some of the operants strengthened are manipulatory and some of their discriminative stimuli consist of the size, distance, weight, and motion of objects; hence, this development is "perceptual-motor." Some of the operants are vocal, as are some of the respondents, and their discriminative stimuli, reinforcing stimuli, and conditioned eliciting stimuli

typically are both objects and the behavior of people; hence, this development is both "cultural" and "linguistic."

4. The processes of discrimination and generalization of stimuli are applied throughout these sequences of development. Thus, the child's operants and respondents may be attached to classes of eliciting and discriminative stimuli. These classes may have varying breadth, depending upon the variety of conditioning and extinction procedures applied to them. Consequently, the child's manipulatory and verbal behaviors seem to deal in classes; this phenomenon, coupled with the complexity of discriminative stimuli possible in discriminating operants, typically gives the label "intellectual" to such behaviors.

5. The equation of discriminative stimuli to secondary reinforcers suggests that many discriminative stimuli will play an important role in strengthening and weakening operant behaviors in the child's future development. Some of these discriminative stimuli consist of the behavior of people (typically parents), and thus give rise to "social" reinforcers: attention, affection, approval, achievement, pride, status, etc. Again the preceding principles are applied, but now to the case of social reinforcement offered for what are therefore "social" behaviors under "social" discriminative stimuli. Hence, the development so described is "social" behavior or "personality."

6. In all of these steps, the scheduling of eliciting, discriminative, and reinforcing stimuli, to one another and to responses, is applied. This gives an explanation for characteristic modes of response which distinguish children: typical rates, the use of steady responding or bursts of activity, resistance to extinction, likelihood of pausing after reinforcement, etc. Deprivation and satiation cycles would see similar application.

Keller and Schoenfeld[1] have written with the same ambition, and have stated the goal as well as we believe possible. Let us conclude, then, as they did:

---

[1] Keller and Schoenfeld, *op. cit.*, pp. 365–66.

The cultural environment (or, more exactly, the members of the community) starts out with a human infant formed and endowed along species lines, but capable of behavioral training in many directions. From this raw material, the culture proceeds to make, in so far as it can, a product acceptable to itself. It does this by training: by reinforcing the behavior it desires and extinguishing others; by making some natural and social stimuli into discriminative stimuli and ignoring others; by differentiating out this or that specific response or chain of responses, such as manners and attitudes; by conditioning emotional and anxiety reactions to some stimuli and not others. It teaches the individual what he may and may not do, giving him norms and ranges of social behavior that are permissive or prescriptive or prohibitive. It teaches him the language he is to speak; it gives him his standards of beauty and art, of good and bad conduct; it sets before him a picture of the ideal personality that he is to imitate and strive to be. In all this, the fundamental laws of behavior are to be found.

REFERENCES

These references contain general discussions of the systematic principles introduced here. The reader who wishes a more detailed discussion of these principles is recommended to read them. Keller and Schoenfeld's text is particularly good in explaining these principles and giving some of the experimental data upon which they are based. Skinner's discussions in *Science and human behavior* are stimulating and valuable in showing how these principles may be applied to complex human behaviors.

Keller, Fred S. *Learning: reinforcement theory*. New York: Random House, 1954.

Keller, Fred S., and Schoenfeld, William N. *Principles of psychology*. New York: Appleton-Century-Crofts. Inc., 1950.

Skinner, B. F. *The behavior of organisms*. New York: Appleton-Century-Crofts, Inc., 1938.

Skinner, B. F. *Science and human behavior*. New York: MacMillan, 1953.

Skinner, B. F. *Cumulative record*, enlarged ed. New York: Appleton-Century-Crofts, Inc., 1961.

INDEX

Anthropology, 9, 12
Associative shifting, 28

Biology, 9, 43

Conditioning,
   classical, 28
   operant, 38, 56
   Pavlovian, 28
   respondent, 28, 56, 81
   S-S, 56
Conflict, 65 ff., 74
Conscience, 78–80

Deprivation, 64–66
Development, 1 ff.
Discrimination,
   operant, 48 ff.
   respondent, 30, 31 ff.
Dollard, John, 49

Ecology, 9
Emotion, 29, 70, 71, 73 ff.
Extinction,
   operant, 39 ff., 51 ff.
   respondent, 29 ff.

Functional relationship, 18

Generalization,
   operant, 48 ff., 57
   respondent, 30 ff.
Gesell, Arnold, 32

History, stimulus, 8, 14, 33, 66
Hull, C. L., 16

Ilg, Frances L., 32
Interaction, 1, 23 ff., 37
Involuntary, 26

James, W. L., 75–76
Jones, Mary C., 30, 75

Kantor, J. R., 17, 24
Keller, F. S., 53

Miller, N. E., 49

Natural science, 3 ff.

Operant, 15, 16, 32 ff., 71 ff.
   discriminated, 49
Operant level, 39 ff.
Operant-respondent relations, 71 ff.,
   76, 81
Organismic events, 10, 11, 12, 17, 72

Pavlov, I. P., 16, 28
Personality, 13, 23, 55
Practice, 47
Punishment, 19, 27, 37, 39, 79

Raynor, Rosalie A., 30